YORKSHIRE MOTORSPORT

A CENTURY OF MEMORIES

LARRY CARTER

AMBERLEY

Front cover: World 500 cc champion Barry Sheene rounds Mere Hairpin at Oliver's Mount, Scarborough, in 1977. (Steve Webster at Mortons Archive)

First published 2024

Amberley Publishing
The Hill, Stroud,
Gloucestershire, GL5 4EP

www.amberley-books.com

ISBN: 978 1 3981 1684 9 (print)
ISBN: 978 1 3981 1685 6 (ebook)

British Library Cataloguing in Publication Data.
A catalogue record for this book is available from the British Library.

Typeset in 10pt on 13pt Celeste.
Origination by Amberley Publishing.
Printed in the UK.

CONTENTS

MOTORSPORT VENUES IN YORKSHIRE

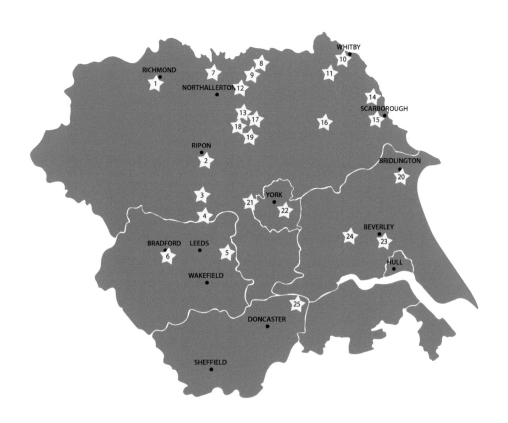

1. 1971 Scott Trial
2. Hutton Conyers
3. 1971 RAC Rally
4. Harewood
5. Ginetta
6. 1986 National Breakdown Rally
7. Croft
8. Woodhouse Farm
9. Carlton Bank
10. Skelder Bank
11. Glaisdale
12. 1938 Scott Trail
13. Boltby
14. Harwood Dale
15. Oliver's Mount
16. Pickering
17. Long Plan Farm
18. Sutton Bank
19. Kilburn
20. Carnaby Raceway
21. Rufforth
22. Elvington
23. Carnaby Two
24. Sancton
25. Thorne

FOREWORD BY STEVE WEBSTER MBE

As a proud Yorkshireman, born and bred, it is an honour to be asked to write the foreword to this wonderful book on the rich heritage of motorsport from our region.

The circuits at Elvington and Carnaby were an integral part of my career in the early days, as well as spectating at Oliver's Mount and watching motocross and grass tracks at places like Sutton Bank, Boltby and Pickering, so much of the content profoundly resonates with me.

Throughout my career, whilst chasing my World Championship dream and being fortunate to win ten of them, the one constant has always been the same, and that is I was always happy to return to my home near York. It meant some very long trips, but it was worthwhile!

I've been lucky to have been surrounded by motorbikes and cars for most of my life and it helped having a dad who was three-times British Grass Track champion. Both me and my elder brother Kevin would attempt to ride the various contraptions we built between us, on two, three and four wheels, but once the bug had bitten, I was determined to race.

I went to Carnaby with a friend called Graham Harrison, and we concocted a plan to start racing sidecars, as they looked like great fun, and having read magazines with the likes of Jock Taylor's and Rolf Biland's exploits featured, that was the route I wanted to go down.

I spoke with my dad, and he said he'd had a similar conversation with Kevin, so we bought an outfit and took it to a local industrial estate to test it out. We hadn't decided who would drive and who would passenger at that point, so we took it in turns and it transpired I wasn't the best passenger and Kevin wasn't the best driver, so that was that sorted!

We did a few club meetings and things were going well, so much so that our sponsor, Paul Seward, bought us a state-of-the-art TZ750 Yamaha engine, but that didn't work out as planned. Kevin and I entered a National meeting at Carnaby in 1981 and because we weren't used to the speed, we had a big accident in which Kevin broke his leg quite badly.

He made a full recovery but it took a while, by which time, with his full support and encouragement, I was forging ahead with my career, which started with winning the 1982 Marlboro Clubman's Championship followed by a couple of British titles and then the first, and in my view the best, World Championship crown in 1987 with fellow Yorkshireman Tony Hewitt.

I was fortunate my career ran right the way through to my final World Championship title in 2004 with Paul Woodhead, with other passengers including Gavin Simmons and David James being part of my successes over the years.

There were fun times along the way, including the sixty-two Grand Prix wins and being awarded the MBE, the painful times with the crash at the 1983 TT and the famous televised encounter with a ditch at Assen! And in a sport tinged with tragedy, I personally know all about that too...

I have fond memories of the battles I had over the years with the likes of Rolf Biland, Egbert Streuer, Alain Michel, Darren Dixon and latterly, Klaus Klaffenböck, Steve Abbott and Tim Reeves which will live with me forever, and reading some of the chapters in this book has invoked some precious memories for me in many ways.

I hope you enjoy the book as much as I have enjoyed my career. It's been a privilege to have been asked to contribute.

Steve Webster MBE
Ten-time World Sidecar Champion
York

Steve Webster (right) chats on the victory lap with commentator Murray Walker as passenger Tony Hewitt soaks it all up. (Ronnie Weir)

CHAPTER ONE

YORKSHIRE WORLD CHAMPIONS

YORKSHIRE'S NUMBER ONES

What do Captain Cook, gunpowder plotter Guy Fawkes, World Cup-winning goalkeeper Gordon Banks, multiple award-winning actress Dame Judi Dench and rock legend David Bowie's dad all have in common?

Correct, all were born in Yorkshire. Perhaps not hard to believe given that the UK's largest county has such an expansive reach, but with other famous Yorkshire folk including former Prime Minister Harold Wilson, loudmouth TV presenter Jeremy Clarkson, cricket legend Geoffrey Boycott, soccer ace Kevin Keegan, acclaimed writers the Brontë sisters, comedian Frankie Howerd, celebrity chef James Martin, comedian Ernie Wise and poet laureate Ted Hughes, the list is as diverse as it is endless and impressive.

And when it comes to motorsport, the region is justifiably proud to boast its own list of successes over the past century.

1958 Formula One World Champion John Michael Hawthorn was born in Mexborough in what was then the West Riding of Yorkshire on 10 April 1929. Mike, as he was commonly known, subsequently spent most of his childhood in Surrey due to his father Leslie purchasing the Tourist Trophy Garage in Farnham, which he later inherited when his father died in a road accident in 1954.

Famed for his blonde hair, pipe-smoking and wearing a bow tie during races, a successful racing career culminated in him becoming the United Kingdom's first Formula One World Champion driver in 1958, whereupon he announced his retirement, having been profoundly affected by the death of his teammate and friend Peter Collins two months earlier in the 1958 German Grand Prix. Hawthorn had also been affected by being involved in the tragic accident which marred the 1955 24 Hours of Le Mans.

Just three months later, he lost his own life in a road accident on 22 January 1959 on the A3 Guildford bypass aged just twenty-nine. He was on his way to meet Collins' fiancée but, suffering from what would have been a terminal kidney illness, it's thought he blacked-out at the wheel. As such, his potential was never realised and with a total of three career World Championship Grand Prix wins, Hawthorn has the lowest number of Grand Prix wins scored by any Formula One World Champion.

Motorcycling has done the white rose county proud over the years with a number of riders tasting World Championship glory. Having started in 1988, the FIM World

Superbike Championship can boast five British riders having won the title, with 40 per cent of them coming from Yorkshire.

Sheffield-born James Toseland won the title for Ducati in 2004 and repeated it on a Honda in 2007, followed by Tom Sykes from Huddersfield who claimed the crown for Kawasaki in 2013, having missed out by half a point the previous season to Italian legend Max Biaggi.

Sidecar racing has long been a bastion of success for Yorkshiremen, headed by none other than Steve Webster, who claimed a total of ten world titles to make him the most successful driver in the sport's history. Born in Easingwold and still resident in York, 'Webbo' won his first world title in 1987 while partnered by fellow Yorkshireman Tony Hewitt whilst his tenth and final crown came in 2004 with another Yorkshire resident, Paul Woodhead, in the chair.

From 181 Grand Prix and World Cup races entered, he has had sixty-two wins, thirty-seven second places and twenty-seven third places, as well as eighty-two pole positions. Perhaps most famously, in 1985 Webster and Hewitt had a massive crash at the Dutch TT at Assen, shown many times on television where the sidecar left the track at high speed, slid along the grass before hitting a drainage ditch. Steve retired in 2005 and as you will have seen, agreed to pen the foreword to this book!

Another sidecar racer who was originally supposed to follow in his dad Peter's saddle and become a jockey is the diminutive Andy Hetherington from the racing village of Middleham in Wensleydale. After a fledgling solo career, Andy ended up as a sidecar passenger after agreeing to step into the breach following a drunken bet one night on the Isle of Man. The next day he was hurtling down Bray Hill at 100 mph in the chair with Lancastrian Dave Holden at the controls...

That was the start of an impromptu but hugely successful career in which he first partnered Leeds motor dealer Eddy Wright to runner-up spot in the European Championship in 1991 followed by an invitation from Darren Dixon to join him. There, the pair culminated a successful partnership with world crowns in 1995 and 1996 before Andy retired in 2002. He is now a window cleaner in Bedale and still proclaims himself as 'the poorest ever World champion'!

Trials aces Dougie and Martin Lampkin's successes are depicted elsewhere in this book, as indeed are those of Malcolm Rathmell, whilst Scarborough's Michael Brown (2007), Jack Challinor from Halifax (2010) and Huddersfield rider Jack Price (2016) are also World Champions.

Silsden stock car aces Frankie Wainman, both Senior and Junior, also chapterised in here, as well as Peter Falding, can boast eight world titles between them. Other Yorkshire World Champions include Richmond's Tony Neal (1968), Stuart Bamforth from Huddersfield (1976), Starbotton driver Mike Close (1977), Rotherham's Willie Harrison (1982) and Paul Harrison from Wickersley in 2011.

And depending on your take as to whether 1992 World Speedway champion Gary Havelock was born north or south of the border-defining River Tees in Yarm, given he's been resident in North Yorkshire for a good part of his life, we will claim him for one of our own for this purpose!

There are others in various realms of motorsport whose achievements are of World Championship status, or at least equivalent to, including Harry Hemingway, who clinched the FIM World Trial 3 title in 2022 to add to a proud list over the years.

Gary Havelock won the World Speedway Championship in 1992. (Sarah Hall)

Yorkshire-born Mike Hawthorn was the UK's first Formula One World Champion. (Cartersport)

Steve Webster and Tony Hewitt in action at Anderstorp in 1988. (Phil Wain)

Sheffield's James Toseland is a two-time World Superbike champion. (Cartersport)

Andy Hetherington (right) partnered Darren Dixon to a pair of world titles in the 1990s. (Cartersport)

CHAPTER TWO

THE LAMPKINS OF SILSDEN

OFF-ROAD ROYALTY

Quite simply, the Lampkins are probably the most famous off-road motorcycle sporting family of all time.

Originally from London, patriarch Arthur Lampkin, along with wife Violet and their two children Janet and Arthur Junior, were evacuated north in 1940 to escape the London Blitz. He worked in a munitions factory at Woolwich Arsenal but was a machine turner by trade and after first arriving in Burnley, he eventually settled in Yorkshire where he opened his precision engineering business.

That home was in the quaint town of Silsden on the northern fringes of the sprawling City of Bradford, and it was in the early 1950s that three brothers would emerge into motorcycling folklore which continues with a fourth generation to this day.

Eldest of the three siblings was Arthur John Lampkin (usually referred to as 'A. J.' in the entry lists) who was born in 1938 and effectively created the Lampkin dynasty. Along with Alan, born in 1944 and affectionately known as 'Sid', the pair were joined at Christmas in 1950 by youngest charge Martin, and between them, they would rewrite the history books when it came to mud-plugging.

All three lads had been around motorcycles from birth with their dad's mode of transport being an old BSA followed by a sidecar, and with the rolling countryside of Craven all round them, it was the ideal territory to hone their off-road skills.

Young Arthur had quickly shown a keen interest in bikes after he was given a 1937 side-valve BSA at the age of twelve and by the time he was just seventeen, he became the youngest ever member of the works BSA off-road team after some inspiring results.

In the end, there was little that A. J. didn't win in the world of trials and motocross. He was a 250 cc and 500 cc GP winner, a member of the British teams in the Motocross des Nations and the Trophee des Nations and represented Great Britain in the International Six Days Trial (ISDT) in both 1958 and 1962 winning Gold Medals. He was also Driver's Stars Champion in the ACU 250 cc and 500 cc classes (the forerunner of the British Championships) and was runner-up in the 1961 250 cc European Motocross Championship.

He was a prolific winner of trials events, with victories in the Scottish Six Days Trial (SSDT) in 1963, the Scott Trial (1960/61/65) and the British Experts Trial. Sadly, despite his best efforts, a World Championship eluded him, but he is probably best remembered as

'Mr Television,' a title he earned from his sterling efforts in the televised winter scrambles of the 1960s.

After Arthur came Sid, again usually listed by his initials in programmes as 'A. R. C.' (which stood for Alan Raymond Charles), who, as well as being an accomplished trials rider, was a highly successful scrambler during the golden era of the 1960s, which saw lots of British domination.

Allegedly, the nickname came about when working in elder brother Alan's motorcycle showroom. One day he was left in charge and ended up selling loads of stock so upon his return Alan recognised the feat by acknowledging his kid brother as 'Sid the second-hand super salesman', and the name stuck.

His first major success was in 1963 when he won his first National trial, the Travers, before going on to win the Bemrose Trophy Trial, the Scottish Six Days and also the Scott Trial in 1966 for BSA. He also enjoyed success at the International Six Days Trial (ISDT) where he won gold medals, and in 1974 won the very first World Trials Championship round to be held in the USA.

Alan continued to ride over the years and competed in his last Scott Trial in 1980 and his last Scottish Six Days Trial in 1982 on an SWM, before handing the reins to his son, James, who was the youngest of his three children who soon became interested in trials riding to follow the family tradition. James went on to have his own successful trials career, which included an Expert British Championship title and a third position in the 2004 SSDT. However, James put his own career ambitions as a trials rider on hold as he supported his cousin Dougie to a number of his World Championship titles.

Harold Martin Lampkin soon followed in the footsteps of his two elder brothers, which included another eponymous programme listing, his being H. Martin Lampkin.

It was inevitable that 'Mart' would soon establish himself as the latest in the Lampkin motorcycling dynasty and by the early 1970s, with the British motorcycle industry in decline, he gained the attention of a certain Francisco Bultó, the owner of the Spanish Bultaco motorcycle company. Bultó offered him a job as a member of the Bultaco factory trials team and in 1973 he won the European Trials Championship, as well as the British National Trials title.

In 1975 the European Championship was upgraded to World Championship status and Lampkin claimed the title to become the first-ever trials World Champion. He continued to experience success on the world scene until 1980, when the Bultaco factory began to experience financial troubles. Lampkin then joined the SWM factory team until he retired from professional competition in 1982.

Besides his European and World Championship titles, Lampkin was also a four-time winner of the Scott Trial (1977, 1978, 1981, 1982), a three-time winner of the British Trials National Championship (1973, 1978, 1980) and won the gruelling Scottish Six Days Trial three consecutive times from 1976 to 1978.

Of course, there soon were bigger fish to fry when his son Douglas arrived on the scene in 1976. As young Dougie grew up and displayed an immense amount of natural talent, Martin supported his son as he embarked on his own phenomenal career.

Loud, larger-than-life but above all incredibly knowledgeable, Martin set the benchmark for first riding and then minding, and his death in 2016 at the age of just sixty-five was a huge loss to everyone who knew him.

Dougie Lampkin MBE, for his whole life, has been intrinsically linked to the sport of trials riding, initially through his famous family connections and later through his incredible achievements which have seen him win an amazing twelve world titles. From 1997 to 2003, he won seven consecutive outdoor titles and five indoor crowns.

Having started riding at the tender age of three, and now in his forties, Dougie is still racking up the wins and recently won his fourteenth SSDT and took a sixth Scott Trial victory. Not many champions go out at the top. The competitive drive needed to win has seen him land those dozen world titles, ninety-nine outdoor wins, thirty-six indoor wins and four Trial des Nations victories coupled with winning everything and anything else within his chosen sport.

He even set a record by completing a lap of the Isle of Man TT course on the back wheel of a trials bike and dabbled in the world of extreme enduros, whilst these days, he is turning his hand to organising and promoting arena trials.

Dougie's brother Harry, his cousins Dan and Ben Hemingway and another cousin John, who was himself a world title contender in the early 1980s and played a huge part in Dougie's early career, were synonymous with one of the most famous sporting names in the world, and the next generation are already stamping their mark, including Dougie's son Alfie who contested his first Scott Trial in 2022, just like their successful ancestors.

Arthur 'A. J.' Lampkin in action on his 441 cc BSA at a televised scramble at Jewels Hill in 1966. (Nick Nicholls at Mortons Archive)

Martin Lampkin on a 250 cc Bultaco
at the National Experts Trial of 1971.
(Nick Nicholls at Mortons Archive)

A rare colour shot of Arthur Lampkin riding the 500 cc BSA at the Hawkstone Park Grand Prix
in 1965. (Nick Nicholls at Mortons Archive)

Alan 'Sid' Lampkin tackles Orgate Falls on the Scott Trial in the mid-1970s. (Tony Todd)

Dougie Lampkin MBE at a slightly deeper Orgate Falls some forty years later. (Neil Sturgeon)

CHAPTER THREE

THE 1971 RAC RALLY

FROM HARROGATE IT STARTED

One of the most iconic events in the past century of British motorsport has to be the annual RAC Rally, which has morphed from one version or another since the inaugural running in 1932.

Then, the Royal Automobile Club Rally, which was the first major rally of the modern era in Great Britain, saw 367 crews entered in unmodified cars, start from nine different towns and cities including London, Bath, Norwich, Leamington, Buxton, Harrogate, Liverpool, Newcastle upon Tyne, and Edinburgh.

In the post-war years, the November classic traversed the halcyon period of the 1950s into the 1960s, where it entered the forests for the first time to host the 'Special Stages', right the way through the golden era of the 1970s and 1980s where the commercial aspect really took hold, and it became almost universally known as 'The Lombard RAC Rally'.

Through the 1990s into the Millennium speed, safety and technology meant a more compact event, which is why, when the UK is occasionally granted a round of the FIA World Rally Championship, these days it takes place over three days, usually in Wales. The purists bemoan this 'nine-to-five' rallying where crews sleep in their own beds every night, mechanics have luxurious service parks to work in, and sterile safety zones preclude spectators from getting anywhere near the action.

It was, however, a totally different story back in the early 1970s and one such event from 1971 stands out because, quite simply, it was the basis for a revolution. That most positive of revolutions was to do with coverage of the event with some of the first ever onboard images and helicopter shots featured by the visionary producer Barrie Hinchcliffe.

It was all part of a new era of broadcast which harnessed the increasing power of television (and radio) whilst emerging from the traditional showreel coverage, typically provided by British Pathe News and without putting too fine a point on it, the techniques were way ahead of their time.

'From Harrogate it Started' is a unique view of the 1971 *Daily Mirror*-sponsored RAC Rally, where teams encountered some of the most extreme weather conditions the event had seen in years. The wintry weather provided a stunning backdrop to the dramatic action, which features crashes, roadside servicing and even one famous team who end up in a lake.

The action features cameras inside the cars, on the stages and from the air as helicopters follow the competitors on long, fast straights and there is plenty of action footage of the very best drivers of the time including the Ford Escorts of Roger Clark, Timo Mäkinen and Hannu Mikkola, with victory eventually going to a youthful looking Stig Blomqvist whose Saab was totally suited to the challenging conditions.

As well as the stunning action and aerial photography, one of the most innovative features is the psychedelic soundtrack which instantaneously transports you back to a gentler, less complicated time. The imaginative narration combines national BBC news reports, including the ongoing exploits of an escaped chimpanzee, with recognisable Radio 1 jingles from the time, and music from The Who, who actually sponsored a car in the event. There are also short excerpts from the old GPO rally reports which you accessed from public telephone boxes to call a number and find out the very latest results and news.

This was from the time when the event itself was the attraction as there was no World Drivers' Championship until 1979 and so the event was simply everything and this film shows what an epic the old-style RAC Rally was. 2,500 miles of which 375 miles were contested on seventy-seven Special Stages over the length and breadth of the UK and not a four-wheel-drive car in sight. Day and night and back into day again, it's how rallying was back then, as witnessed by the hundreds of thousands of fans who lined the route.

From the Harrogate start, stages in Yorkshire which feature in the documentary include Esholt Water Works in Bradford, Harewood House and Bramham Park near Leeds, and Castle Howard near Malton, followed by traversing 6-inch-deep snow in the Yorkshire forests before heading into even worse weather further north.

'The toughest night in the history of the RAC Rally' was how one competitor described it, with Roger Clark quipping 'Everything has gone white'! The film captures intrinsic details such as the early morning sun glinting off icicles in a brook, frozen and snow-covered marshals just this side of hypothermia, a pair of frogmen ready to assist any unfortunate competitor who ends up in the sewage works and even a competing Austin Maxi! Incidentally, the reward for the fastest driver through the Bradford sewage works went to Hannu Mikkola, whose prize was a pair of hand-made suits...

It's only half an hour long but the film really was the pathfinder for modern rally coverage and perhaps the defining image was when Yorkshireman Peter Clarke and co-driver Tony Mason, later to accompany Roger Clark to victory followed by an illustrious television career presenting *Top Gear* and their famous Rally Reports, crashed their 1600 cc Ford Escort into a lake at Woburn, before being dragged out by a pair of RAC Land Rovers.

For the record, Blomqvist and co-driver Arne Hertz's winning time was seven hours 30.47 seconds, just over three minutes ahead of fellow Swedes Björn Waldegård and Lars Nyström in a Porsche 911S. Third were Carl Orrenius and Lars Persson, also from Sweden, in another Saab 96 with Finnish driver Hannu Mikkola and co-driver Gunnar Palm taking fourth in their Ford Escort RS1600. The similar car of teammate and compatriot Timo Mäkinen, with British co-driver Henry Liddon, were fifth with the Lancia Fulvia of another Finn Simo Lampinen and co-driver John Davenport in sixth.

Finn Simo Lampinen and co-driver John Davenport in a snowy Langdale forest in their factory-entered Lancia Fulvia 1.6 Coupe HF. (Tony Todd)

Nigel Hollier and Bryan Coyle in their Birmingham Post-backed Renault Alpine A110 on SS4. (Tony Todd)

The wintry conditions didn't suit the unusual Ford Capri of Michael Bennett and Eddy Bamford. (Tony Todd)

County Durham driver Fred Henderson at the start of Langdale in the Mini Cooper S he was sharing with John Lee. (Tony Todd)

Yorkshire hopes rested with Tony Fall and co-driver Mike Wood in their Datsun 240Z, but sadly they crashed out. (Tony Todd)

CHAPTER FOUR

SUTTON BANK AND HAREWOOD HILL CLIMBS

RUNNING TO THE HILLS

With the invention of the motor vehicle at the turn of the twentieth century, soon came man's desire to pit their fledgling machines against each other and after the uncertainties of the early years, where the limits of the internal combustion engine and its derivatives were found, ways and means were being explored to extract competition.

Notwithstanding the First World War and with racetracks being virtually non-existent, it was public roads which lent themselves to man and machine fighting it out, with hill climbs particularly popular as the gradients added an extra element to the intensity.

The more daunting the better and one such place, which is still a sizeable challenge these days to the regular road user, is Sutton Bank. Linking the main A170 between the Vale of York and the North Yorkshire moors, the road climbs 160 metres in under 1 mile. The bank has three sections of steep 1:4 (25 per cent) inclines along its length and just over halfway up is a left-hand hairpin bend. Near the top, there is a final short steep section before the main road bends sharply right.

The very nature of Sutton Bank deterred car clubs from attempting climbs in the early years so it was left to the motorcyclists to uptake the challenge. The earliest organised time trial on the bank was held in 1908, before in 1919 Teessider Freddie Dixon, on a 7-bhp Indian, set a record of 1 minute 22.2 seconds for the climb.

The first recorded climb by cars was in May 1914 when competitors had two runs with records showing S. Rollason (Singer) beat the AC of S.C. Westall on both climbs. Post-First World War, it was the turn of York and DMC to organise an event in August 1920, when HF Clay's American-built Essex made the best time of 1 minute 58.6 seconds. Meetings were moved to springtime, and in April 1921 Archie Frazer Nash set the fastest time of 1 minute 21.6 seconds driving a self-built Godfrey Nash (GN) cycle car. The GN was a lightweight two-cylinder car where Frazer Nash's racing successes in highly developed versions of the cars contributed to their popularity.

However, the locals weren't happy with the road being used for competition, and in the summer of 1921, farmers had successfully petitioned Thirsk Rural Council to 'prohibit the use of Sutton Bank for other than legitimate purposes of passing to and from the towns to which it leads'.

But a counter petition was presented to the council which led Cllr A. Pearson to state: 'These motors bring in a fair amount of money, which is distributed between the hotels and the tradespeople of the district. The slight damage to the road and the small amount of inconvenience is outweighed by the advantages.'

Thus, the council agreed that for one day only each spring, the hill climb up the famous road could continue, and in May 1922 Leeds driver Harry Hodgson won the 1500 cc and unlimited classes in his self-designed Anzani with a time in the wet just 10 seconds slower than Frazer Nash's previous best.

By now, the popularity of the sport was catching on and a reputed 15,000 people attended the meeting in April 1923 despite the wet conditions, which made the hill muddy and treacherous. Therefore, it was not surprising that the cars were faster than the motorcycles with J. H. Clay taking fastest time in his Vauxhall Velox 30-98 open tourer to win.

But it wasn't to last, and the final meeting took place in April 1924 in torrential rain so heavy the number of motorcycle classes had to be abandoned with the road coated in thick mud. Despite the conditions, it was E. R Hall in his 1500 cc Aston Martin who made best time of the day.

Another famous hill climb, although not a public road, is that of Harewood. Located just outside of Leeds in the Wharfedale valley, Stockton Farm came on the market in the early 1960s after the BARC had been looking for a hill climb course for some time. Lifelong member and owner of the famous tailoring chain Arnold Burton bought Stockton from the Harewood Estate and gave the club the right to improve the roads and hold events.

Members set to work on building the course ready for the first event in September 1962 where Tony Lanfranchi set the fastest time of 51.61 seconds in his Elva Mk6 Climax. The initial success was followed in 1963, but the June meeting saw scorching temperatures, which led to the surface melting. That meant a race against time to repair the road for the British Championship event in September, which went ahead as planned with Peter Boshier-Jones setting a new record at 46.72 seconds.

The BARC Yorkshire Centre continues to run Harewood Hill climb, which is the longest speed hill climb course in mainland UK totalling 1,440 metres with the fastest time set in July 2022 by Wallace Menzies in his 3.3-litre Gould GR59 at 47.97 seconds.

Teesside rider Freddie Dixon on his Indian Scout from 1920 after setting the Sutton Bank hill record the previous year. (Mortons Archive)

A postcard from the very early days showing the paddock at the descent of Sutton Bank with the daunting hill in the distance. (Cartersport)

Peter Westbury sits patiently at the bottom of Harewood Hill climb awaiting his turn at a 1964 meeting. (Cartersport)

Motorcycle competitors tackling the steep 1:4 gradient around a hundred years ago. There's a lot more foliage on Sutton Bank nowadays! (Cartersport)

The roads around Stockton Farm at Harewood have been used many times on the Lombard RAC Rally. Here's Stig Blomqvist on the 1974 event. (Terry Wright)

CHAPTER FIVE

THE 1938 SCOTT TRIAL

HAPPY ANNIVERSARY - GREAT SCOTT!

Back in 1938, there was an air of gloom and despondency hanging over the world as a bloke called Adolf Hitler was doing his best to batter the free world into submission. In September of that year and having been named *Time Magazine*'s 'Man of the Year', the Führer met with three other statesmen in Munich to redraw the map of Europe as the world barrelled inevitably towards war again.

British Prime Minister Neville Chamberlain, Premier Edouard Daladier of France, and Benito Mussolini of Italy were deemed the only world figures of importance to Hitler and, with the Anglo-French policy of appeasement meaning Czechoslovakia was sold up the river to join Nazi-annexed Austria, the 'Munich Agreement', signed by both Hitler and Chamberlain, guaranteed 'peace in our time'. And we all know what happened soon afterwards...

However, a month or so after the most insignificant document of the twentieth century was signed, a group of people were gathering under those impending clouds of war with a contrasting outlook, in the hope things may not turn out as bad as expected.

After twenty years of being based in the West Yorkshire Dales near Bradford, the Scott Trial celebrated its coming-of-age in the North Yorkshire foothills for the first time. With new custodians Middlesbrough and Stockton Motor Clubs, both then in the North Riding of Yorkshire before the boundaries were redrawn in 1974 and placed into the new Cleveland county, it was sure to be a hard act to follow on territory which, in many cases, hadn't seen any motorised activity before.

The world's toughest one-day trial was to be based in Carlton-in-Cleveland under the jurisdiction of Clerk of the Course Jack Gash, who must have wondered what he'd let himself in for when a massive storm arrived on the Friday and rendered much of the planned course impassable. As the various officials sought shelter in an Osmotherley hostelry, the question was asked of Mr Gash as to how much of the course would be lost in the deluge? 'Not an inch of it, it's got to be done' came the curt and comprehensive reply. And he was true to his word.

Luckily, the storm blew itself out overnight, so, on Saturday 19 November 1938, eighty entrants converged on the start in trepidation of what lay ahead. Well, that was apart from a few local competitors who'd taken the opportunity during the preceding week to have a walk around the suspected route to fill them with even more dread.

One in particular was F. M. Rist of the Tanks Corps who was a professional rider in the Army. Fred to all that knew him, he was a local rider from nearby Stokesley and made his name both pre- and post-war in competitive motorcycling of all disciplines. So serious was he about making a good impression now the Scott Trial was to be held in his proverbial back yard, he took a whole week's leave to foot-slog over the moors in a bid to suss out the probable course. At around 20 miles a lap, that took some doing…

With bright sunshine greeting the riders, they were flagged off from a farmhouse in Carlton and headed through uncharted territory. As these magnificent men on their fledgling machines negotiated the natural obstacles, one such section was to ride down a steep descent into Scugdale Beck, traverse the swollen stream, and exit up a muddy slope the other side. A vast crowd had gathered to witness the spectacle, which didn't disappoint as many competitors took an unscheduled dousing in the freezing water.

Onwards they battled with names such as local aces E. G. Pipe, A. W. Armstrong, T. Whitton, and J. H. Wood to the fore before the big guns started to show their colours. Allan Jefferies, whose son Nick and grandson David went on to become major TT stars, survived the treacherous Ryan's Folly section. So too did Fred Rist and the fancied Vic Brittain behind early pace-setter Len Heath.

The course skirted Sheepwash, the Drover's Road and Chequers public house before arriving at Black Hambleton where competitors had to cross the road and view civilisation (people!) for the first time since they set off. A steep climb up the hill and then back down it saw Heath continue to head the field through sections such as Cringle Wood and Carlton Bank to end lap one.

Such was the going that only half the field survived that first lap and with darkness rapidly approaching, the ghostly moors were deemed too dangerous for them to continue. One poor rider, A. T. Johnson, broke his ankle and had to be carried a mile over moorland on a farmer's gate to receive assistance.

The retirements continued as Vic Brittain went out with an injured foot and other tales of woe included bikes held together with billy band and a certain K. D. Haynes attempting to ride with snapped handlebars. He didn't succeed and was left on the exposed hills until 9 p.m. before he was found.

At 3.30 p.m., some 3 hours, 28 minutes, and 44 seconds after he started, Len Heath averaged 14.37 mph on his 497 cc Ariel to set Standard Time and with forty-eight marks lost on observation, he landed the coveted Alfred A. Scott Trophy, twelve marks ahead of J. H. Wood. Fred Rist was third as just seven riders were initially classified as finishers, although the timekeepers allowed an extra half hour which encompassed another thirteen.

At the Middlesbrough Motor Club clubhouse, Councillor Swales presided over the awards ceremony where a decent sum was raised for the St Dunstan's charity. Heath cut the twenty-first birthday cake which he was presented with and made sure the organising clubs got a big slice as they had overseen the transition of the event to its new home and made it a resounding success in the process, despite the weather.

Sadly, it was another eight years before the wheels of competition would again turn due to the onset of hostilities which Mr Chamberlain had promised wouldn't happen, but the Scott Trial re-emerged in the Cleveland Hills in 1946 and stayed there until 1950.

Fred Rist, on his 499 cc BSA, claimed third place on the 1938 Scott Trial. (Mortons Archive)

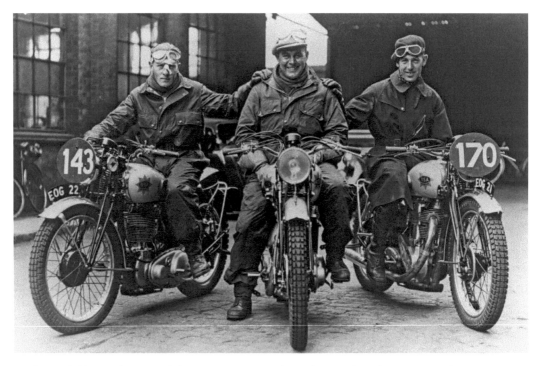

Fred Rist (left) was also part of the 1938 ISDT team from the Royal Tank Corps, seen here with Gold Star teammates R. Gillam and J. T. Dalby. (Mortons Archive)

Above left: The Scott Trial hazards were no less daunting pre-Second World War. (Mortons Archive)

Above right: The cover from the very rare 1938 Scott Trial programme. (Cartersport)

An old picture from Sheepwash and the Drover's Road near Osmotherley which formed part of the Scott Trial course in 1938. (Raphael Tuck & Sons)

CHAPTER SIX

THE LOST CARNABYS

FROM BOMBERS TO BIKES

Northern England, in fact much of the flatter eastern part of the UK, is littered with airfields or airstrips, of varying size and shape, some still operational, some long gone. A quick blast on Google Earth will reveal many ghostly clues to runways past, some of which form industrial estates, some continue as airfields, and some have succumbed to housing developments or agriculture.

Many were hastily built just before or during the Second World War to accommodate the increasing air power needed to successfully defeat the enemy and after hostilities had ceased, and operations wound down, many were abandoned or fell into disrepair.

RAF Carnaby near Bridlington in East Yorkshire was one such place whose primary role was as an emergency landing strip which offered crippled or low on fuel bombers a safe place to land near the English coast. It opened in March 1944 under the control of No. 4 Group Royal Air Force and unlike most RAF airfields, there was a single runway, five times the width of a standard one and 9,000 feet (2,700 metres) long.

It served its purpose as over 1,500 bombers made an emergency landing at Carnaby by the end of the war. It was one of the pioneering airfields operating the fog dispersal system known as FIDO (Fog Investigation and Dispersal Operation). FIDO consisted of two rows of pipes, one on each side of the runway, that burned petrol. The heat from the flames cut a hole in the fog and provided crews with a brightly lit strip indicating the position of the runway.

The base closed in 1946 but was reactivated in 1953 for a year due to the need to train pilots for the Korean War. Thereafter, from 1959 to 1963, it became a PGM-17 Thor intermediate range ballistic missile base and housed defensive Bloodhound surface-to-air missiles.

By 1969 Carnaby had closed altogether, yet this was still not the end for this remarkable place as two local authorities purchased the site in 1972 for it to become an industrial estate, and one of its early origins was as a storage facility for the newly imported Lada cars.

Such was the vast expanse of the site, the derelict land at the western end of the site and wide runways were an ideal venue for the Auto 66 Club, based in nearby Driffield, to run motorcycle and kart races as well as car sprints so a lengthy period of negotiation commenced. It took a long time to procure the necessary planning and operational permissions but on Sunday 3 August 1975, the inaugural meeting took place at Carnaby with another meeting the following year and then another couple in 1977.

But it wasn't until 1978 that things really took off, and such was its success further meetings were planned for 1979. The 1.5-mile track had a surface that was a mixture of concrete and asphalt and was quite bumpy in places. The facilities were virtually non-existent with temporary toilets, race control in a caravan and because of its location just 3 miles from the North Sea, a freezing cold wind was usually in evidence.

Into the 1980s and entry lists often boasted over 350 solo competitors and seventy sidecars and under the guidance of the late visionary Peter Hillaby, the track was given a new name of Carnaby Raceway and developed to attract the bigger championships. The car and kart element became minimal and national motorcycle events featured regularly, as well as the staple of club racing.

The end of season Carnaby Bonanza saw many top names attend including future World 500 cc champion Wayne Gardner, but without doubt the highlight was the British Championship meeting in May 1988, which was televised live by BBC Grandstand over two days, with the late, great Murray Walker providing commentary. The only other live coverage provided by the BBC was the British Grand Prix, so it really was a coup for the organisers.

Sadly, that was to be the swansong as at the end of that season, the existing lease expired and although plans were afoot to build on the success and revenue generated from the TV rights and exposure, the council had other ideas and refused to renew the lease.

Thus, a short but exciting tenure had come to an end and at the end of 1988 the circuit closed. These days, a visit to the industrial estate sees it has expanded and some parts have encroached into the confines of the old circuit, although it is still possible to make out the old profile of the track.

But that wasn't the end of Carnaby, as the controlling Auto 66 Club tried to resurrect the original version at their 'Carnaby Two' venue at RAF Leconfield near Beverley just over a decade later. Originally planning to replicate the shape of the switchback layout, it was developed into a track which featured the names of some Auto 66 Club stalwarts on corners as tributes. It ran from 2001 to 2004 before the Defence School of Transport (DST Leconfield), which was now operational on the site, needed to add street furniture as part of their training programme, which meant it wasn't suitable to continue racing there.

Factory Suzuki GB riders Keith Huewen and Paul Iddon competed in the 1982 Carnaby Bonanza meeting. (Michael Dowkes)

Hornsea rider Phil Usher claimed the Count of Carnaby title in 1981 on his 500 cc Suzuki. (Michael Dowkes)

Scotsman Eric McFarlane leads Paul Iddon in a Production race at Carnaby in the late 1970s. (Michael Dowkes)

Whilst bike racing was the predominant activity at Carnaby Raceway, karts and occasionally cars took to the track. (Michael Dowkes)

Yorkshireman Geoff Johnson in action on his 600 cc Honda at the BBC televised meeting in 1988. (Alan Horner)

CHAPTER SEVEN

CHRIS MEEK

THE ADOPTED YORKSHIREMAN

Juxtaposed with Farnham, whereas 1958 Formula One World Champion Mike Hawthorn was born in South Yorkshire before moving there, Chris Meek was the opposite in as much as he was born in the Surrey town before making his home in West Yorkshire.

It was from his Leeds base that he became the stereotypical Yorkshireman; bold, brash, straight-talking and one hell of a racing driver in some of the most iconic and inventive cars of his generation.

Born Christopher John William Joseph Meek on 21 December 1932, he went on to study in Leeds before starting racing motorcycles in the mid-1950s. Chris began his racing career on four wheels in 500 cc Formula 3 with a car which he dubbed 'The Meek Emperor', its first recorded appearance being at the Brough circuit in East Yorkshire in 1956. He soon switched to sports car racing with Lotus Types 9 and 10 followed by an Alfa Romeo Giulietta Sprint Veloce and an Elva Courier.

With the Elva, Chris won the 1960 Gold Flake Trophy at Phoenix Park in Dublin. A return to single seaters saw Chris racing the Formula Junior Elva 300, including a crash at Goodwood which hospitalised him, before switching his allegiance back to sports cars in 1964, joining the Walklett Brothers in Leeds where they built Ginettas, and equipped with a special 'works' G4 he enjoyed considerable success at national level.

In the late 1960s, after an abortive spell in Formula Three, Meek entered a number of 1600 cc Formula Two events, but his cars were uncompetitive, and his only classified finish was ninth in the BARC 200 at Thruxton with a Brabham BT10.

After a few races with a Chevron-BMW B8 as a member of the TechSpeed team, Chris moved into Formula Ford 1600 with a Titan Mk 6 entered by his company Titan Properties Ltd, which he ran for over forty years. In 1970 with the Titan and in 1971 with a Tate of Leeds-sponsored Lotus 69F Chris won the BRSCC Northern Formula Ford Championship. The Tate support continued into Formula Atlantic with a Brabham BT38, a March 712 and then a Motul M1, Chris winning a British Championship round at Snetterton.

One of the stars of Formula Atlantic was a young Welshman by the name of Tom Pryce whom Chris decided to support through his flourishing company, arranging for Tom to drive a Motul for Ron Dennis's Rondel Racing team. At the end of the year Tom won the premier Grovewood Award. After a few F1 races with the Token RJ02 and victory in the Monaco F3 race in 1974, Tom became much sought after and signed for the Shadow team.

Chris, meanwhile, was continuing to race extensively, principally in production sports cars such as a De Tomaso Pantera, some ultra-fast Lotus Europas, a TVR 1600M, MG Midget, Panther Lima and even an ultra-rare Costin-Nathan. Between 1973 and 1980 Chris won six production sports car championships.

With period flared trousers, flowery shirt and the long, unkempt hairstyle of a pop star, there was usually a stereotypical gold bracelet and giant medallion around his neck. He suffered fools badly and had more than the odd run in with over-zealous officials, which would see him storm away from a race meeting.

Meek was renowned for his style and flair, which was epitomised by the eclectic mix of sponsors that used to adorn his various steeds. Princess Ita was one, testimony not to an ancient Egyptian king's daughter who lived in the twelfth dynasty around 1850 BC, but allegedly a female acquaintance as well as the trendy pirate radio station Radio Luxemburg with its medium wave broadcasting frequency of 208 being used as his race number.

His cars were always very reliable and immaculately prepared, usually trailered behind a ubiquitous 3-litre Ford Granada Estate. One of his original faithful mechanics was Pete Riches, who subsequently went on to become the technical guru for the BTCC, and even had a corner named after him at Snetterton.

Chris Meek exits Railway Straight at Croft after doing a parade lap on a motorcycle. (Tony Todd)

One of his high-profile girlfriends was Biba model Valerie 'Valli' Stack, whose name first came to prominence in motorsport circles in 1975, when she was photographed sunbathing topless near the lake at Mallory Park and the pictures were published in the British motoring press! Chris persuaded Valli to try her hand at racing and she took to it like a duck to water, claiming some good race finishes and a string of lap records too. She raced between 1975 and 1977, driving an MG Midget, Lotus Europa, and Triumph TR7, usually under the characteristic black and gold colours of the fashion house Biba.

In the early 1980s, Chris reduced his racing activities and instead, via Titan Properties, he acquired the freehold of the troubled Mallory Park circuit in Leicestershire in 1983. Always a colourful, flamboyant character, Chris owned in excess of forty Ferrari road cars over the years and also had a succession of fast road bikes. He is alleged to have driven one of his Ferrari Enzos at a speed of 217 mph – the model's top speed – but refused to say where and when it happened!

Meek achieved more than 500 race wins during his illustrious career and gained the highest number of lap records of any other driver at the time. Latterly, very few knew of his charitable work for deprived children in Russia, his wife Svetlana's homeland.

A very colourful character who was incredibly kind and generous and who left an indelible mark on Yorkshire motorsport, Chris sadly died in 2016 after a long fight against cancer.

Meek at the wheel of the Princess Ita-sponsored Ford Escort at Rufforth. (Tony Todd)

The unique De Tomaso Pantera was another one of Meek's steeds, seen here at the Croft chicane. (Tony Todd)

The Skoda was one of the less famous cars Meek drove, but with stereotypical 1970s hairstyle and pose in the Croft pits, the picture tells the story. (Tony Todd)

CHAPTER EIGHT

THE CARTER FAMILY

TRIUMPH AND TRAGEDY

Despite the obvious connection with the author, the name of Carter is one steeped in Yorkshire motorsport tradition, but one family in particular has inked their indelible stamp on the sport.

Incredible successes were tempered with unimaginable tragedies which left a heart-wrenching legacy and the same desire that drove them to the heady heights of being the best in the business proved to be the demons that effectively destroyed them.

Headed up by Halifax car dealer Mal Carter, the larger-than-life character whose generosity knew no bounds as his Pharaoh Garages concern set the likes of Phil, Terry, and Ron Haslam on their way to stardom. A mountain of a man, he talked as much with his fists as he did with his mouth and despite his outgoing generosity, he was an overpowering presence on those around him.

Two of his sons were Kenneth, born in March 1961, and Alan, who came along in August 1964, whereby both would become successful motorcyclists in their own rights, despite in very different disciplines of the sport. And whilst not quite achieving their own world championship titles they so richly deserved, they came mightily close.

But tragedy was a constant just about from the off in the lives of two seemingly ordinary Yorkshire lads who shared an unrelenting passion for success. Firstly, there was their loving mum, Christine, who glued the tempestuous family together. Aged just twenty-six and with youngest son Malcolm in tow, she set out on a journey on Saturday 24 October 1970, but a puncture caused her to crash the Ford Cortina she was driving leaving her with life-changing injuries. Worse still, four-year-old Malcolm died the following day from chest injuries in Halifax Infirmary.

In Pinderfields hospital for a year and subsequently bed-ridden with paralysis from the neck down, Mal then left Christine and filed for divorce, which meant her remaining two sons had to care for her as best they could, but as with any kids of such age, it had a profound and lasting effect on both Kenny and Alan. Life went on and Kenny in particular immersed himself in motorbikes, given he was surrounded by them through his dad's involvement with the sport. Both he and Alan continued to look after their mum, who by now had remarried. But alas, nine years of pain, torment and sheer hopelessness took its toll and Christine took her own life three months short of her thirty-sixth birthday.

Rocked by the double tragedy of losing their younger brother and now mother, both Kenny and Alan knew only one way to deal with such devastation, and that was to totally focus on their two-wheeled careers. For all his faults, Mal ensured that both lads had the very best equipment and by now, Kenny was becoming established as a half-decent speedway rider.

Aged just seventeen, he started his shale career with Newcastle Diamonds in 1978 before signing for his hometown club Halifax Dukes, for whom he rode until 1985. During that time, he qualified for the 1981 World Final run before 92,500 fans at Wembley Stadium. He finished fifth that year and repeated the result in 1982 in Los Angeles after a controversial Heat 14 exclusion following a coming together with defending champion, and eventual 1982 winner, arch-rival American Bruce Penhall in which Carter fell and was excluded. Kenny finished fifth again in 1983 at Norden in West Germany, the same year that he become World Pairs Champion with Peter Collins.

'King' Kenny also won the British League Riders' Championship in 1981 and 1982 and was British Champion in 1984 and 1985 but had to sit out the 1985 World Final at the Odsal Stadium in Bradford after breaking his leg in the Intercontinental Final in Sweden.

Often outspoken, he signed for Bradford Dukes in 1986 before another fateful twist in the Carter story unfolded. A deeply troubled twenty-five-year-old Kenny, with the legacy of his mum and younger brother still haunting him and coupled with the frustrations and injuries of his career, wrongly believed that his wife and childhood sweetheart Pam, also the same age, was cheating on him. On Wednesday 21 May 1986, he shot her dead at their luxury farmhouse in Bradshaw and then killed himself, orphaning their two young children in the process. The couple were controversially buried together and their simple gravestone at a cemetery in Bradshaw bears their names, their date of death and the names of their children.

Whilst Kenny's speedway career was burgeoning, so too was younger brother Alan's in the world of motorcycle racing. Quickly rising through the national ranks, he became, at the time, the youngest winner of a Grand Prix race when he took the French 250 cc race in 1983 aged just eighteen on his World Championship debut.

He couldn't manage to replicate that success, although his best season came in 1985, when he finished seventh in the 250 cc World Championship and went on to compete in 54 GPs until 1990. He won on his debut at the North West 200 in 1994, raced successfully in the British 250 cc Championship and latterly in World Superbikes, as well as a successful stint in the USA. No one doubted he had the talent to go all the way to the top but failed to fulfil his enormous potential for numerous reasons.

Perhaps it was the stormy relationship in the early days with his domineering father, and former manager, Mal, the tragic death of his young brother and the suicide of both his mother and his elder brother and untimely death of his sister-in-law all had an effect. So too did his failed business deals and bankruptcy in the financial crash of 2008 after a large number of customers went bust on him. That cost him his home, along with the personal struggles that saw him turn to religion for salvation, but perhaps the one event which affected Alan the most, and the one he's most candid about, is the loss of his own baby daughter.

It happened after his racing career had ended when partner Carmen was giving birth on 8 January 2002. Sadly, baby Charlie died during childbirth to compound yet another tragic milestone in the Carter household.

These days, 'Mighty Mouse', as he was nicknamed during his career, is an established rider coach, helping with the careers of a number of up-and-coming stars in motorcycle racing, with names such as Ryan Vickers, Ben Luxton, Korie McGreevy, the late Chrissy Rouse, Eugene and James McManus amongst others, winning numerous championships along the way.

Alan (left) and Kenny Carter, at the height of their careers in the early 1980s, pose for a pre-season photoshoot in the hills above Halifax. (Alan Carter)

Alan Carter, seen here at Donington Park in 1983, was the youngest winner of a Grand Prix when he took victory in France the same year. (Nick Nicholls at Mortons Archive)

Above left: Kenny Carter was cruelly denied a World Speedway Championship title during his short career. (Alan Carter)

Above right: A youthful Kenny in his early days riding for his hometown club, Halifax Dukes. (Cartersport)

Mal Carter (right) was a major sponsor of many riders, including shaping the early career of Ron Haslam (left). (Nick Nicholls at Morton Archive)

CHAPTER NINE

MICK GRANT

TRUE YORKSHIRE GRIT

City or United, Rangers or Celtic, Spurs or Arsenal, in football terms, some choices are more clearly defined as you can only be one or the other.

Back in the mid-1970s, there was a similar choice when it came to motorcycle racing: the ultra-successful Cockney charmer Barry Sheene, who was sweeping all before him in a flamboyant age of World Championship racing, landing two 500 cc titles on the bounce, or Mick Grant, the genial Yorkshire working-class hero with a spit-and-sawdust attitude to match.

Sheene's good looks and multicolour Suzuki leathers contrasted with bearded and moustachioed Grant in his plain lime green and white Kawasaki suit, and whereas Sheene was bordering on cocky with his southern rhetoric, Grant said precious little, or sometimes 'nowt' to coin a famous Yorkshireism...

In truth, those were the apparent personas of each man, who wholesomely embraced the characters they were perceived as, but in truth they were good mates. Their seeming rivalry divided fans, but it made sure that crowds flooded through the gates in support of one or the other, and in doing so made more than an odd healthy pay day for each of them!

Michael Grant was born at Wetherby in July 1944 and began his competitive career on a 350 cc Velocette at Baiting's Dam hill climb in 1965. After a few off-road events, he made his road racing debut at Croft in 1965 on the same Velocette. His first victory came a few years later in 1969 at Cadwell Park, which was the same year as he entered his first Manx Grand Prix on a 500 cc Velocette where it's recorded that he finished forty-eighth – and last!

Undeterred, his first TT was the following year, again using the Velocette and placing eighteenth in the Junior 350 cc class on a Yamaha TD2 with an average speed nudging 90 mph before his career really started to take off in 1971 when he won a national race at Cadwell Park before taking his first international victory at Scarborough.

Grant initially received support from Peter Padgett from Padgett's of Batley on TD2 250 cc and TR2 350 cc Yamahas, and then Brian Davidson of the John Davidson Group on TZ Yamahas, but he was equally versatile on either two-stroke or four-stroke machines. He usually raced with number ten and carried the initials 'JL' on his helmet as a tribute to his early sponsor, mechanic, fabricator, and frame-builder Jim Lee, who latterly built the Dalesman trials bikes.

Mick quickly rose through the ranks to become a works Norton rider alongside Peter Williams and Phil Read, and in 1972, he teamed up with Dave Croxford to win the Thruxton 500 endurance race on a 745 cc Norton Commando. He claimed his first TT podium with a third place in both the Senior and Junior TTs, behind the legendary Giacomo Agostini, and won again at the Scarborough International to give Norton their first Superbike victory.

1973 saw the hat-trick of wins at Scarborough International completed on a JPS Norton in a season which saw Grant take to the world stage with a best result of fourth on a 250 cc Yamaha at Assen. Another season in Europe followed in 1974 but the highlight was Mick securing his first TT victory on a 750 cc 'Slippery Sam' Triumph in the Production race.

At the end of the year, Grant was the chosen rider for the new, UK-based, Boyer Kawasaki Racing Team, based on the factory's air-cooled triples, and 1975 became the first of a four-year tenure on the 'Green Meanies'. That year, Mick completed the first ever 120 mph lap of the North West 200 circuit on his way to victories in both the 500 cc race and the main NW200 race. That same year, it was Grant who finally broke Mike Hailwood's absolute TT lap record set in 1967, raising the average speed to 109.82 mph on a Kawasaki KR750 two-stroke triple. Although Grant failed to finish the race, retiring at the Gooseneck, he won the 500 cc Senior TT race and topped the season off with being crowned British Superbike champion.

By now Grant's rivalry with Barry Sheene was intense but he missed out to the Londoner in the 1976 British Superbike Championship after a tough season, which saw him again combine domestic races with international duties for Kawasaki. He made up for it somewhat in 1977 by taking his first GP wins in the 250 cc class in both Holland and Sweden, whilst raising the TT lap record to 112.77 mph and winning the end-of-season Macau Grand Prix. Sadly, he couldn't follow that up in 1978 where his best result was third in the 350 cc race at the washout British Grand Prix.

1979 saw Grant move to Honda to help develop their exotic oval-cylindered NR500, but despite some occasional encouraging results, mostly the project was unsuccessful and the picture of Grant sliding down the track on his backside on the opening lap of the 1979 British Grand Prix, before the 'Never Ready' burst into flames, adorns the front cover of his wonderful autobiography *Takin' the Mick*.

By now, the light was starting to fade on a fantastic career, or at least it seemed that way. Despite his advancing years, Grant still managed to remain competitive, winning the 1980 Formula One TT and the British Formula One Championship, whilst finishing runner-up in the World Formula One Championship.

He won again at the 1981 North West 200 and TT before moving to Suzuki GB for 1982 where he finished fourth in the World and third in the British Formula One Championships, respectively. Similar results prevailed for 1984 in the same series, where he also added a second Macau Grand Prix victory and by 1985, in his fortieth year and final one in competition, Grant won his last TT race as well as taking victory in the burgeoning new British Superstock Championship. And just for good measure, he finished runner-up in both the British and World Formula One Championships.

After hanging up his leathers, Grant went on to manage the Suzuki British Championship team and oversaw the early career of the likes of James Whitham and Steve Plater amongst others and played a part in the resurrection of Oliver's Mount in the 2010s. Still looking half his age, Mick still competes regularly in trials, which he openly admits has always been his true passion when it comes to motorcycles.

Green Meanie! Mick Grant on the 750 cc Kawasaki at Mallory Park at the TransAtlantic Match Races in 1978. (Nick Nicholls at Mortons Archive)

Grant (right) with Dave Aldana (left) and Barry Sheene after finishing on the podium in the 1975 Race of the Year at Mallory Park. (Nick Nicholls at Mortons Archive)

After leaving Kawasaki, Grant rode for Honda and won the British Formula One Championship and TT in 1980. (Ronnie Weir)

Deep in thought and sporting the trademark moustache. (Phil Wain)

At the age of forty, Grant won the 1985 British Superstock title for Suzuki before he announced his retirement. (Phil Wain)

CHAPTER TEN

THE OFF-ROAD TRACKS

YORKSHIRE'S SCRAMBLING HERITAGE

The county of Yorkshire is home to its fair share of motocross tracks, some still active, some sadly not, and at one time you could barely go a week without there being a motorcycle meeting hosted in North Yorkshire.

Thirsk and District Motor Club was founded in 1949 and since then has hosted motocross – or scrambles as they were then known – as well as hill climbs, trials and enduro events. In the early days of the club, they even managed to organise closed-road hill climbs up Sutton Bank long before it was the busy highway we know today.

They also used to use a track around Lake Gormire, at the foot of Sutton Bank, where they ran races on Boxing Day. Thirsk and DMC initially ran scrambles in Boltby Forest, which had been used by motorbikes since 1945. Back in the 1960s these events were televised nationally, and the television crews were struggling to get a broadcast signal out of Boltby.

So, several of the club's members, including Bob Hunter from Thirlby and Sutton-under-Whitestonecliffe resident John Thompson, took on the challenge of seeking a new venue where the signal would be easily obtained, but they wanted it to remain close to Boltby.

They headed to Long Plain Farm on top of the Hambleton Hills to speak to farmer and landowner Tom Cornforth, who as a motorsport fan made no hesitation in offering options to Thirsk and DMC, originally giving them the choice of an old quarry in an arable field before realising that an undulating grass field containing a tricky quarry would probably make a great course.

One condition of use was that Tom got to meet top rider and two-time European Motocross champion Dave Bickers when he visited his farm, and the rest is history as they say. The course remains in the same location that the club runs their motocross events at today.

Famous commentators attended the motocross events in the region in the 1960s and 1970s including Murray Walker, and top rider Alan Lampkin, as well as Bickers, would ride there. Police had to steward the meetings back then due to the huge crowds attending. Sadly, Tom passed away in 1970 but the relationship between Thirsk and DMC continued with his son Derek, and granddaughter Amanda, who are both rally competitors and motorsport enthusiasts, and still does today.

The club also continued running motocross meetings in Boltby forest with both Boltby and Long Plain hosting rounds of the Haynes Four Stroke Championship in the late

1980s and early 1990s. Some of the sport's top names would attend including British Championship runner-up Jared Smith, Mason Weir, Mark Fulton, Steve Howell, BSB team boss Paul Bird and former World champion Jeff Smith.

In 1989 Thirsk and DMC teamed up with Northallerton and District Motorcycle Club to host the penultimate round of the British Championship in Boltby, attracting many fans and top riders at the time. Now Thirsk and DMC usually run two motocross events a year and a couple of trials at Long Plain Farm, as well as trials at nearby Kilburn. They originally ran the Kilburn hill climb before Pickering Motor Club took over the organising of the annual summer event.

Thirsk and DMC have also produced some champions as well. Dennis Teasdale was the British Grass Track Sidecar champion in 1981 whilst Paul Teasdale was the Under-21 British Motocross champion in 1996. Kilburn's Ian Cartwright went on to be a successful speedway rider at Halifax Dukes in the late 1970s and early 1980s also.

Nearby Pickering and District Motor Club continue to host events and as well as running the Kilburn hill climb, they have two courses they use at Wrelton and Haygate Lane where they organise up to five events in each discipline, including grass track, trials, hill climbs and motocross. Their member Rob Bradley, from Slingsby near Malton, has also been British Grass Track Sidecar champion on four occasions and is still competing.

Whitby Motocross Club was formed in 2000 after the demise of the Langbaurgh Motocross Club at Glaisdale. Former members of the club refused to see the sport disappear from their area and found new land to run events on at Skelder Bank near Whitby. In 2005 they were approached to host a round of the British Championship, an opportunity they jumped at, and they continue to host high level events today for British Championships and at a national level.

Hutton Conyers near Ripon was another venue that used to see events televised. Run by Ripon Motor Club, after thirty-four years the track was shut down in the early 2000s reportedly after complaints from neighbours and also some historic artefacts being found on the site. The club is more renowned for organising trials, but it hosted motocross events at Hutton Conyers including the North versus South competition and the Yorkshire Grand National, which were televised in the mid-1990s.

Scarborough and District Motor Club were fortunate enough to be gifted land and own their course at Low North Park in Harwood Dale, near to the seaside resort. They hosted motocross events there up until around the year 2000 and now it is only used for trials.

Hull and District Motorcycle Club would run races at their course at Sancton near Beverley in rotation with the East Yorkshire Association clubs – Scarborough, Thirsk and Pickering – meaning there was a constant stream of competition with virtually a meeting on every weekend and club and regional championship spoils to be taken.

Over the years, however, many tracks have sadly gone by the wayside and have long since disappeared back into the scenery from where they rose. Northallerton and District Motorcycle Club used to host motocross at Carlton Bank, near Stokesley, Woodhouse Farm at Great Ayton was used by the Langbaurgh and Northallerton clubs, Nether Silton is no more whilst there was a club at Thorne near Doncaster who had three different venues, but sadly they are no longer used.

There were also venues at Whenby, near Brandsby in North Yorkshire, and at Terrington Bank. There has been a rise in recent years of courses that can be hired and used for practice and competitions such as Topcliffe, Dalton, Gale Common and Wilberfoss.

Bryan Wade rides the bumps at Boltby in the early 1970s. (Tony Todd)

Blast off at Boltby as the field roars away from the start. (David Bell)

The famous downhill jump from High Paradise at Boltby with the starting gates in the background. (David Bell)

Thirsk & District Motor Club Ltd.

NORTH v SOUTH TEAM MOTO CROSS

Long Plain Course, Nr. Sutton Bank

OFFICIAL PROGRAMME 30p.

SUNDAY 11th MAY

For conditions of admission - see inside.

Programme cover from the North vs South team meeting at Long Plain Farm in 1986. (Cartersport)

The start at Hunter's Hill Farm, Nether Silton, from 1975, which used to host scrambles. (Tony Todd)

CHAPTER ELEVEN

OLIVER'S MOUNT, SCARBOROUGH

SEASIDE SPECIAL

Most of us have enjoyed a day out at Scarborough. For me, it was the go-to family holiday destination in the 1970s, where lazy days on the beach would be curtailed with a first house sitting at a show at the Futurist or the Floral Hall theatres. Tourists thronged in their thousands before the cheap foreign holiday package boom took over and condemned the traditional British seaside holiday to a long, painful death.

But the Yorkshire resort is also a little-known mecca for motorsports. Glance up to above the Spa in the South Bay and you will see the war memorial, which is situated on Oliver's Mount. Supposedly named after Oliver Cromwell, who had visited the town in the seventeenth century, the narrow, tree-lined slopes overlooking the coastal town have been hosting hugely popular motorcycle races on the closed roads for over seventy years.

England's only natural 'road' racing track, the origins lie with the enthusiasm of members of the Scarborough and District Motor Club, who began searching for a venue to hold road racing in the mid-1930s. Their first idea was for a 14-mile course at Seamer Moor with another option being to use the town's former horse racing venue nearby to create a 10-mile course, but nothing came of either proposal before the onset of the Second World War.

When peace was restored in 1945 the club renewed its efforts and, with the support of the ACU and the local council, began a search for a new venue. With post-war austerity, costs were now a major factor, so a much shorter circuit was now favoured. Oliver's Mount on the southern edge of the town quickly seemed favourable and plans for the 2.410-mile course were soon laid out.

The circuit was officially opened in September 1946 with the first race meeting following a few days later. Over 12,000 spectators attended two days of racing on Tuesday 17 and Thursday 19 September where Midlander Sid Barnett won both 500 cc events with Yorkshireman Denis Parkinson victorious in the 350 cc race. Bradford's Allan Jefferies and Stokesley rider Fred Rist were also competing.

The original course followed the same layout as today, though for the first two meetings the start was located in the middle of today's Esses at the top of Quarry Hill before being relocated to its current position at Weaponness Farm. Modifications were made for subsequent meetings, including widening the straights and a slight easing of Mere Hairpin. In 1947 racing was transferred to Fridays and Saturdays before the first Sunday meeting took place in May 1971.

The races were popular with the public too, and from 1947 the BBC began radio broadcasts, some of which featured father-and-son commentary duo Graham and Murray Walker, the latter of course going on to find fame as the television voice of Formula One.

Improvements continued over the years including a complete resurface in 1973, by which time the events were under the jurisdiction of Scarborough Racing Circuits Ltd. Big name riders such as Geoff Duke, Eric Oliver, John Surtees, Bob McIntyre, Mike Hailwood, Giacomo Agostini, Jarno Saarinen and Phil Read brought huge crowds, with an estimated 50,000 in attendance at the 1977 meeting.

A big Oliver's Mount supporter, Barry Sheene had just won his second 500 cc World Championship that year for Suzuki and was set to do battle with Yorkshire crowd favourite Mick Grant on his lime-green Kawasaki. Sheene set a new lap record in the first clash before retiring but in the MCN/Brut 33 British Superbike Championship race over fifteen laps the pair went at it like men possessed in the early laps, roared on by the partisan 60,000 crowd. When the Sheene machine stopped again, it not only compounded a miserable weekend for the Londoner, but it also left Grant to claim another victory in front of his adoring fans.

The circuit continued to host British Championship races throughout the 1980s with big-name riders including Wayne Gardner, Graeme Crosby, Steve Parrish, Keith Huewen and Roger Marshall, but the increasing speeds came to a head in 1989 when future quadruple World Superbike champion Carl Fogarty lapped the course at an average speed of over 82 mph, including three walking-pace hairpins. Something needed to be done so a new chicane near the start/finish area was installed in 1991.

1996 saw the fiftieth anniversary celebrations with a record crowd of over 63,000 to see their heroes from yesteryear, who could between them boast thirty-two World Championships. The star line-up included fifteen times World Champion Giacomo Agostini reunited with his former factory MV Agusta, Jim Redman on the Honda-6, Barry Sheene on a Suzuki RG500 and Carl Fogarty on his Honda RC45.

In 1999 a new pedestrian footbridge was built over Quarry Hill, and further improvements and safety work carried out but by now, the track had fallen out of favour with many riders as it no longer hosted the main championships. It did, however, continue to attract the leading TT riders including John McGuinness, Michael Dunlop, David Jefferies, Ian Hutchinson, Dean Harrison and Ian Lougher, as well as a certain Guy Martin. Indeed, the side-burned TV presenter and part-time racer is the most successful having won eight Gold Cups between 2003 and 2012.

A couple of high-profile accidents in 2017 saw members of the public injured, which led to a safety review and meant racing could not continue until the recommendations were carried out. That spelled the end for the existing organisers but with the backing of Scarborough Borough Council, a new consortium including former racers Mick Grant and Eddie Roberts oversaw the return of racing in 2019, which, now under new ownership, has continued despite the pandemic difficulties in recent years.

Hill climbs and sprints on two, three and four wheels are part of the circuit's heritage, as well as hosting stages of car rallies, such as the Lombard RAC. Latterly, it was pedal power which took centre stage in 2016 when the parkland hosted a classified climb in the Tour de Yorkshire.

For an iconic and unique track, and having raced there myself on two wheels, and rallied on four, I can vouch first-hand it offers a challenge like no other. Long may it continue as that's the least this venerable old lady deserves.

A union flag sidecar start at Oliver's Mount in front of the packed banking. (Michael Dowkes)

John Cooper (JC) and Barry Sheene (2) head up Quarry Hill in the early 1970s. (Nick Nicholls at Mortons Archive)

Barry Sheene, seen here at Mount Hairpin in the mist of 1978, was a regular visitor to Oliver's Mount throughout his career. (Michael Dowkes)

Rallying featured regularly with cars usually going the opposite way to the bikes. York's Tony Drummond tackles Mere Hairpin on the 1975 Mintex Rally. (Rally Retro)

YORKSHIRE CENTRE A.C.U.
President: T. E. FLINTOFF, Bradford & D.M.C.

OPEN RACE MEETING
FOR MOTOR CYCLES
AT
Olivers Mount, Scarborough

Tuesday, September 17th, 1946
AND
Thursday, September 19th, 1946
Commencing each day at 10-30 a.m.

Held under the International Competition Rules of the F.I.C.M. & the General Competition Rules of the A.C.U.

Open Permit No.: A.C.U. 63
Temporary Track Cert. No.: 361

Run in conjunction with the SCARBOROUGH & D.M.C.

OFFICIAL PROGRAMME Price, ONE SHILLING

The programme cover from the very first race meeting at Oliver's Mount in 1946. (Cartersport)

CHAPTER TWELVE

THE 1986 NATIONAL BREAKDOWN RALLY

LET IT SNOW

There used to be a time when high-performance projectiles reverberated through forest tracks at all times of the day and night with the echo of horsepower rebounding off the trees as thousands of eager spectators lining the roads watched in awe.

Special Stage rallying was massive, as showcased by the annual jaunt around the UK in the guise of the Lombard RAC Rally and one conservative estimate by the organisers one year was that around six million people had watched the event at some point during the five-day (and night) marathon.

It didn't matter that it was 4 a.m. in the depths of Kielder Forest, in sub-zero temperatures with a 3-mile walk to get to the action, as the sleet turned to snow. You had slept in the car for two nights already but a rally jacket, a bobble hat and a flask of soup was all you needed. And a load of equally excited mates to await the action.

Of course, growing up in North Yorkshire with its riches of forest locations, most of which were revered in rallying folklore, it was difficult not to get bitten by the rallying bug. The likes of Dalby, Cropton, Gale Rigg, Langdale and Wykeham were staple tests on many events and nearer to home, the likes of Silton, Boltby, Wass, College Moor, Deer Park and Ingleby were lesser used but no less daunting.

Sadly, with the march of progress coupled with environmental and health and safety pressures, despite the sport upping its game considerably, especially in the safety ranks, it's hard to believe that there are a diminishing number of events planned these days. OK, Covid-19 did its best to wreck the sporting industry in the UK, but nonetheless, the future is anything but bright for British forest rallying.

Some thirty-eight years ago, that wasn't the case and one such event that stands out was one of the many times I was stood in the middle of nowhere at some unearthly hour. The unforgettable 1986 National Breakdown Rally.

It was late February, and the event comprised the opening round of the British Open Rally Championship, which was a vitally important marketing tool for the manufacturers, even if their thoroughbred rally cars bore little resemblance to the road version cousins. The four-wheel-drive revolution was well underway with fire-breathing 400 bhp 'Supercars' as the traditional two-wheel-drive brigade hung on, making for an interesting spectacle all round.

With one of the major motoring organisations backing the rally, which started in Bradford at 10 p.m. on the Friday evening, the plan was to incorporate a handful of 'spectator stages' into the vast amount of mileage undertaken in the battlegrounds of the fast-flowing forests of the Yorkshire Moors. It was to be a virtually non-stop endurance test of man, team and machine incorporating 260 stage miles over the weekend, with the weary crews expected at the Bradford finish on Sunday lunchtime having had the total sum of two hours rest during that time.

But it didn't quite go to plan. There had been a lot of snow in the run up to the event, necessitating snowploughs to clear the stages in the days preceding, and there was a worrying forecast of more heavy white stuff over the weekend. So, with all eyes on the weather and snow starting to fall in the opening two stages of Bowling Park and Harewood House, the crews arrived at Boltby just after midnight.

It was Finn Mikael Sundstrom and co-driver Voitto Sylander who led in their Peugeot 205 T16 ahead of the MG Metro 6R4 of Welshman Dai Llewellin and Yorkshire co-driver Phil Short. Third was the slow-starting winner from the previous year, Hannu Mikkola and fellow Finnish co-driver Arne Hertz in their short wheelbase Audi Quattro S1 as they briefly serviced in the car park at the top of Sutton Bank.

The cars then slithered through stages in Wass and Deer Park just after 1 a.m. as snowflakes the size of footballs fell (as I was there and can vouch!) and subsequently closed the A170. After negotiating a 10-miler in Cropton at around 3 a.m., it was becoming apparent to officials the event as planned could not continue.

A chaotic service area in Pickering saw the experienced Clerk of the Course Jon Sharpe announce to crews that the next loop of stages were impassable, so the remaining competitors were re-routed to the tests in Guisborough and Ingleby forests, which reportedly had nearly a foot of snow in them. Sundstrom still led by a minute over Mikkola as more stages were cancelled amidst the chaos.

Following an impromptu three-hour rest halt in a transport yard in Pickering, the cars were despatched back into battle as the sun rose. A couple of forest stages near Thirsk completed first thing, it was on to the spectator stages at Lightwater Valley and Croft where the fans had turned out in their thousands. The tarmac at both venues resembled a skating rink and it was at Lightwater that Sundstrom, with a two-minute lead, hit a tree, which ripped a wheel off the 205 causing instant retirement.

Mikkola slithered around Croft to set fastest time equally with the Metros of Llewellin and Jimmy McRae, but the weather once again closed in and it became clear the remaining stages, apart from a second run through Ingleby which was next up, would have to be canned. Another rapidly convened meeting between competitors and organisers saw the possibility of two runs through Dalby meaning those two stages would comprise the last two of the event late on Saturday night.

And as it transpired, they were pivotal as Llewellin held a ten-second lead over Mikkola going into the final test only to stall on a hairpin and the resulting time loss saw him lose out to the Finn, who crossed the Bradford finish ramp in the early hours of Sunday morning, 16 seconds to the good. McRae claimed third ahead of the two-wheel-drive Opel Manta 400 of Russell Brookes.

It turned out to be a triumph over adversity in the most extreme conditions as one of the organisers quipped afterwards that the rally should be renamed 'The Nervous Breakdown Rally'. It's such a shame that events like this, once commonplace all over the UK, have fallen victim to modernisation. Much of me wishes they hadn't.

Jimmy McRae and Ian Grindrod battle through the deep snow in their MG Metro 6R4 on the Friday night. (Jonathan Smith – Environmental Media)

Saturday dawned brighter with still lots of snow for Harri Toivonen and Neil Wilson, but they ended up crashing out on the ice at Croft. (Jonathan Smith – Environmental Media)

The driving snow caused major problems, as seen on the front of the Ford RS200 of Mark Lovell and Peter Davis as they eventually finished fifth. (Andy Ellis)

Eventual winners Hannu Mikkola and Arne Hertz thread their powerful Audi Sport Quattro through the slippery narrow roads of Lightwater Valley. (Andy Ellis)

Frozen marshals check in local ace Steve Bannister and co-driver Dave Oldfield, who overcame the conditions to finish fifth overall. (Andy Ellis)

CHAPTER THIRTEEN

CROFT'S ARISTOCRATIC CONNECTIONS

THE NEW BEGINNING - CROFT, PRINCESS DIANA, AND LORD LUCAN...

It seems strange that two of the world's most fascinating and enduring aristocrats ended up having a very tenuous association with Croft but when the racing circuit reopened in 1964, little did anyone know that at the time.

Although there had been motorsport activity at Croft (originally called Neasham) Aerodrome in the fledgling years just after the Second World War, it wasn't until April 1962, when the Air Ministry offered around two-thirds of the land totalling 160 acres for sale at a public auction, that things really started to take off.

A group of mainly local enthusiasts decided that it would make an ideal and much needed motor racetrack to serve the North East so 'The Croft Consortium' as they were known made a successful bid at public auction before seeking planning permission. This was granted in August 1963 and in January 1964, they formed a company called Croft Autodrome Limited.

Thus, Teesside shipbuilding tycoon Sir Robert Ropner was elected chairman. His son Bruce and nephew John – who were both established racers – became directors along with Bruce's (lifelong) friend and fellow racer Keith Schellenberg. Another established competitor, the Hon. John 'Jock' Leith, was also elected to the board with the legal representation being provided by C. S. Tilley (of local solicitors Tilley, Bailey & Irvine).

That only left one more director: a certain W. Shand Kydd. Like Keith Schellenberg and Bruce Ropner, who were British Bobsleigh champions in 1956 and 1962 respectively, Bill Shand Kydd embraced the trappings of his privileged upbringing by becoming a businessman and an adrenaline-fuelled sportsman including being a prolific winter sports athlete, hence the association. He also went on to be a successful amateur jockey and racehorse breeder.

For nineteen years his older half-brother Peter was married to Princess Diana's mother, Frances, after her divorce from Earl Spencer in 1967. But perhaps a more controversial link is that of his brother-in-law, John Bingham, 7th Earl of Lucan – Lord Lucan to most of us. There are various accounts of what happened to lead to his mysterious disappearance, but Shand Kydd was seemingly a prominent figure in the final exchanges between the two.

But all that was in the future and more importantly at the time was to get the first race meeting organised under the new regime. And so it happened when Darlington and

District Motor Club hosted the very first meeting of the new order on August bank holiday Monday in 1964 for the Daily Mirror Trophy.

The format of the meeting was cars, solo motorcycles, and sidecars, which was to become the staple format of the 'Battle of Britain' meetings to follow over the next few years. Reports had between 45,000 and 50,000 fans in attendance and upon police advice, practice and racing was delayed to allow everyone in.

Once up and running, the twelve-lap race for the Glovers of Ripon White Rose Trophy and the £40 prize money was won by Liverpudlian Robin Smith in his Ford Lotus Cortina. Next up was a twelve-lap scratch race for Grand Touring Cars, which saw future Croft legend Chris Meek from Leeds take the victory in his Ginetta G4 with John Ropner, in cousin Bruce's Shelby American Cobra, a notable fourth.

The feature race over twenty laps for the Daily Mirror Trophy saw a titanic battle between late replacement driver Chris Summers (Lotus 22) and pole position setter Julian Sutton from Hexham in his Lotus 23. The pair battled throughout before Summers, from Coventry, took the lead with a new lap record on the penultimate lap and hung on for the £150 first prize.

Sutton got revenge by taking victory in the final event for Sports Racing Cars whilst in the bike ranks, sadly no results are evident, but the entry included future star Dave Croxford (496 cc Matchless) and Middlesbrough's William 'Ginger' Hawthorne (499 cc BSA/Norton). The sidecar contingent saw future British champion Jeff Gawley, Yorkshire bike and car dealer Colin Appleyard, Tynesider Geoff Bell and 'the fastest Geordie on three wheels' Mac Hobson also in action.

Local dignitaries and officials cut the ribbon to open Croft Autodrome in 1964. (Terry Wright)

Part of the Croft Consortium was Keith Schellenberg, seen here manhandling his mighty Bentley. (Tony Todd)

The opening meeting in 1964 featured plenty of aerial activity including a parachute drop and a flypast by the RAF. (Tony Todd)

Luxury safety equipment such as rollover hoops and quite often seat belts weren't required in the early days... (Tony Todd)

EVENT 5

Daily Mirror TROPHY RACE

20 LAP SCRATCH RACE FOR SPORTS/RACING CARS AND RACING CARS OF UNLIMITED CAPACITY

ENTRIES

No.	Driver	Entrant	Car	c.c.	Town	No.	Driver	Entrant	Car	c.c.	Town
47	D. L. Wragg	Wood Lane Garage	Mallock U2 Mk.IV	1498	Sheffield	58	W. A. Robson	Driver	Cooper Junior	997	Darlington
48	J. L. Romanes	Driver	Brabham	1498	Edinburgh	59	W. J. Forbes	Driver	Lotus 23B	1594	Aberdeen
49	T. Dawson	Driver	Lotus 22	1650	Elland	60	J. J. Bouckley	Driver	Cooper Mk. III	1594	SuttonColdfield
50	J. R. Pearce	Auto Racing Service	Lotus 22	1594	Sutton Coldfield	61	J. Cordingley	Driver	J. B. W. Maserati	2500	Haslingden
51	A. C. Goodfellow	Driver	Cooper-Ford	1100	Falkirk	62	W. B. Barton	Entwistle & Walker Ltd.	Lotus 19	2500	Bolton
52	J. Sutton	Driver	Lotus 23B	1594	Hexham	63	J. Rutter	Driver	Aston Martin DB3/5	2992	Newark
53	J. W. Snowdon	S. N. Snowdon	Merlyn Mk. V	1098	Carlisle	64	M. Owen	G. R. Baird	Lola-Buick	3500	West Bromwich
54	M. T. Chipperfield	Driver	Lotus 20	1100	Salford	65	V. A. Wilson	Chamaco-Collect	Lotus 21	1498	Walkington
55	E. A. Worswick	Driver	Lotus 7	1480	Burnley	66	A. Bateman	L. A. Miles	Jaguar 'C'	3442	Wick
56	W. J. Stein	Wm. Stein & Co. Ltd.	Lotus 23B	1594	Edinburgh	67R	R. B. Cochran	Driver	Lotus 7	1340	Burton on Trent
57	R. J. Prest	Driver	Elva FJ	992	Durham	68R	D. Kearsley	Driver	Lotus 7	1498	Chorley

AWARDS

Race winner: "Daily Mirror Trophy" and £150

2nd cash or award value	£75
3rd cash or award value	£50
4th cash or award value	£25
5th cash or award value	£15

The entry list for the 1964 Daily Mirror Trophy Race at Croft Autodrome. (Cartersport)

CHAPTER FOURTEEN

TONY SUGDEN

THE LASTING LONGEVITY OF 'SUGGY'

Many people have put Yorkshire well and truly on the international motorsport map but perhaps none more so than Tony Sugden, who was born in Bradford before making his home in Doncaster. He forged a fifty-two-year career, starting on two wheels before making a name as one of the best Special Saloon car racers in the UK.

Affectionately nicknamed 'Suggy', his record over that half century of competition is quite remarkable and rumour has it, he had to build an extension to his home to accommodate his amassed trophy collection.

Before he started racing cars, Tony enjoyed a number of seasons racing bikes, which started in 1951 on a Triumph Twin and lasted until 1953. A modest start was followed by a year's National Service before returning with a BSA Gold Star when in 1955 and 1956 he racked up the first wins of what was to be an illustrious motorsport career.

1957 saw the arrival of a Manx Norton where over the next three years, he won twenty-two races at various northern tracks including at places like Mallory Park, Cadwell Park and even the defunct Alton Towers, where the circuit wended its way around the famous country house which is now the backdrop for the popular theme park it has become in recent times. He also contested the Manx Grand Prix.

Sugden liked the Alton Towers track and won on eight occasions, including breaking the lap record in 1957, circulating at an average speed of just 51 mph, such was the swervery and tight nature of the course. One of his rivals during that time was a young Phil Read whom Tony beat, netting the grand sum of £19 in prize money!

As the 1960s arrived, Sugden switched to AJS machinery where he posted another eight victories but by now the car bug was biting and after purchasing a Lotus Cortina, he started sprinting and hill climbing, winning over a dozen races.

His circuit racing career started in 1968 with the Cortina but realising he needed more powerful machinery; he purchased a crash-damaged Ford Escort Twin Cam in 1969 and went on to take a total of fourteen class wins over the next couple of years. A 2010 cc version was obtained for the 1971 and 1972 season, which resulted in eleven more victories but it was the mighty Ford Escort BDX which gave him many of his successes.

From 1973 to 1976, Sugden won thirty-six races including three saloon car championships and was runner-up in three others before continuing his success the following year in 1977 with a BDX version, which added another thirteen wins to his increasing tally. A modest season in 1978 saw him briefly venture into the sports car realm with outings in a BDX-engined DAF Volvo and a Jim Price Haulage-sponsored Chevron B23 with just a couple of wins along the way before it was back to the Special Saloon class for 1979 in one of the most iconic cars seen in the sport.

Using the Chevron as a base and taking a basic two-door family Skoda saloon coupe of which over 56,000 were built by the Czechoslovakian manufacturer AZNP in Kvasiny, the rear-engined, rear-wheel-drive car was transformed into a space-framed silhouette with the trusty Ford BDX planted in the middle. The resulting Skoda 110R Super Saloon saw Tony win four titles over the next three years courtesy of over fifty wins, including many at Croft where he'd by now become a firm favourite at the Yorkshire track.

The radical contraptions continued into the 1980s when Sugden continued his winning ways in an A. E. T. Lotus Esprit Turbo. By now, turbocharging was becoming prevalent and Tony Taylor, of A. E. T. Engineering, was pioneering its use in Special Saloon car racing. So, in a bid to promote his business, he and racing driver Jim Evans commissioned a chassis to be built by Yorkshire farmer-come-engineer John Leek, Jim's longstanding mechanic, along with Tony Tait, who looked after the technical side. They then had a fibreglass body of a Lotus Esprit made by Richard Jenvey and fitted an FVA Cosworth 1.6 litre engine to it, to which they added a turbocharger.

The result was four more seasons of success with Sugden claiming another twenty-three victories, which culminated in the 1982 BRSCC Championship. A slightly different version of the car was used from 1985 to 1987 with sixteen more victories coming, but the relationship with John Leek spawned Sugden's final and perhaps most impressive creation.

The Leek Skoda 1993T was a 500 bhp behemoth which Sugden campaigned starting in 1988 right the way up until his retirement in 2003. It featured a Leek monocoque chassis constructed from sheet aluminium with the large inner panels fabricated by Chevron. It sported March 761 and 762 Formula One suspension and brakes, 17-inch-wide rear tyres with a Hewland FGB/C gearbox ahead of a four-cylinder Ford Cosworth engine. With a Garrett turbocharger force-feeding it, Sugden reckoned it had around 500 bhp on the normal 1.8 bar boost, with another thirty or so on tap with a twist of the knob if needed.

Over the years, Leek's commitments meant he no longer had the time to service the car, so Sugden and wife Rose, as chief mechanic, assumed the task and during the final sixteen years of his career, and well into senior citizenship, Tony added an amazing 130 additional wins to his tally.

Basic mathematics determine that over those amazing fifty-two years, Sugden competed in 1,052 races, winning 318 of them and being placed on the podium on another 604 occasions. That is some record for a driver who epitomised the spirit of club-level motorsport. In later years, Tony could be found behind the wheel of the safety car at a variety of circuits before passing away in early 2024.

Tony Sugden had lots of success in his early days driving the BDX-powered Ford Escort.
(Tony Todd)

The same Ford Escort at Rufforth sporting loyal long-term sponsors Brook Hire of Liverpool.
(Tony Todd)

Sugden is synonymous with Skoda, seen here in an early version of the 110R from 1979 at Croft. (Terry Wright)

The radical turbocharged Leek Skoda Super Saloon had lots of Formula One technology included and produced over 500 bhp. (Tony Todd)

List of Drivers and Entrants (continued)

No.	Name & Town	Machine & Entrant	c.c.	Int. Lic. Nos. Driver	Entrant
64	GRANT, H. Kinrardime on Forth	Norton Tom Rutherford	350	Z5015	61/E2074
65	LEIGH, G. E. Southport	Norton G. E. Leigh M/Cycles	348	Z2752	61/E1677
66	SUGDEN, T. Doncaster	A.J.S. Self	349	Z2543	—
67	LAUNCHBURY, F. W. J. Wimbledon, S.W.19	Norton Raynes Park M/Cycles	348	Z2620	61/E1698
68	BULLOCK, J. Clitheroe	Norton Tom Robinson	348	Z2672	61/E1692
69	BANCROFT, M. Horsforth	A.J.S. Bill Bancroft	349	Z5115	61/E231
70	SHAW, A. E. Birkenhead	Norton Self	348	Z2375	—
71	PALMER, G. Pontefract	A.J.S. Self	349	Z5061	—
72	STRACEY, J. F. Isleworth	A.J.S. Joke Equipe	349	Z2783	61/E2027
73	SOMERS, J. St. Albans	Norton Joke Equipe	348	Z2278	61/E2027
74	STORER, N. Chaddesden	Norton Harry Middleton	348	Z2786	61/E1684
75	HOBSON, M. Newcastle-on-Tyne 4	A.J.S. T. Cowie Ltd.	349	Z5195	61/E364
76	KING, D. Bexleyheath	Norton Self	348	Z2607	—
77	COOPER, J. H. Derby	Norton Wraggs of Sheffield	348	Z2862	61/E2011
78	GREENFIELD, D. J. Birmingham	Norton Denis Parkinson	350	Z2413	61/E2001
79	WRIGHT, S. Barnsley	Norton Self	347	Z5201	—
80	FISHER, A. Widdrington	Norton G. Bell (M/Cycles)	348	Z3992	61/E2089
81	HARTLE, J. Chester	Norton Comerfords Ltd.	348	Z2315	61/E1670
82	FLACK, A. J. London, W.5	A.J.S. Self	349	Z4022	—
83	BRETT, J. London	Norton Reg Dearden	349	Z5236	61/E1652
84	INGRAM, R. Rode	Norton Reg Dearden	348	Z2866	61/E1652
85	COLLIS, G. Southampton	B.S.A. Self	349	Z2938	—

8

The entry list for the motorcycle race meeting at Oliver's Mount in 1961 saw Sugden (66) up against John Cooper (77), John Hartle (81) and Mac Hobson (75). (Cartersport)

CHAPTER FIFTEEN

DENIS PARKINSON

THE ULTIMATE PRIVATEER

Sometimes, what someone does after their career has finished has more of a bearing on how people remember them and in the case of Denis Parkinson, that could well be very much the case.

For whilst the record books show him as one of the leading lights in the relative infancy of motorcycle racing, with an impressive set of results which anyone would be proud of, it was latterly his instantly recognisable voice which many associated him with.

Denis Jack Robert Parkinson was born on 13 June 1915 at Wakefield and was only nine years of age when he took the ferry from Liverpool to his beloved Isle of Man to watch the 1925 TT races. It spawned a love affair with the place which saw him return as fan, racer and then radio and television broadcaster over the next sixty-four years.

He first rode in the Manx Grand Prix in September 1932 where the regulations stated then that every entrant driver shall be a 'male person over the age of 18 years'. Do the mathematics and what is for sure is that Denis Parkinson was not of the prescribed age, but nonetheless he finished in both Junior and Senior races riding the same 350 cc machine, which was an excellent result for one so young.

In 1933 he again finished in both races, and he also rode in 1934 and 1935 without achieving any notable success before deciding his apprentice days were over. At the time there was in the Junior event, a race within a race, as there was a special category for Lightweight 250 cc machines.

Parkinson proceeded to make this class his own private property and won the Lightweight class three times in succession in 1936, 1937 and 1938. He also rode the Senior race of 1937 finishing thirteenth and got another replica to add to his fast-growing collection. This replica was the third in the same year, a feat no one had ever done before or for that matter has ever done since in the Manx Grand Prix series.

There was no race in 1939 and after the Second World War in 1946, Denis returned and finished third in the Junior and fourth in the Senior. He won the Junior in 1948 and in the next three years was respectively fourth, third and eighth in the Senior Manx Grand Prix. In 1953 he won the Senior at a record speed on his Featherbed Manx Norton and in the process became the first man to lap at over 90 mph in the Manx Grand Prix.

In practising and racing, he lapped the TT course a total of 388 times, covering a distance of 14,647 miles. In addition, Denis set record laps on four occasions and was twice a member of the winning team and won a total of fifteen replicas.

Denis also won the Clubman's TT and had innumerable success on short circuits notably at venues such as Scarborough and Brough, and in all won over 600 awards. When he retired from racing, he went into officialdom as an ACU Steward, as well as becoming a travelling marshal in the Manx Grand Prix for many years.

But with the increasing popularity of radio and television, which was timed perfectly to coincide with Denis' retirement, he was soon in demand to provide broadcast duties at various events. As well as at the Isle of Man, his voice could be heard at places like Scarborough (where he remained as press officer up until his death in 2004) but it was the hugely popular television scrambles of the 1950s, 1960s and even into the 1970s where his dulcet tones could be heard. His fairly broad Yorkshire accent, combined with an eloquent delivery and intimate knowledge of the sport, was just what the various producers wanted, and he was a regular fixture in many people's living rooms every weekend as the events were beamed live.

He was aged eighty-eight when he died and in his final years, such was the esteem in which he was held in the Isle of Man, that the Manx Government honoured Denis with a commemorative postage stamp in 1993. A fitting tribute to the man who was described as the ultimate privateer.

Denis Parkinson gets congratulated after his first Lightweight Manx Grand Prix victory in 1936. (Mortons Archive)

A picture from 1952 of Denis Parkinson on the Manx Norton. (Mortons Archive)

A poster depicting Parkinson's success at the 1953 Manx Grand Prix. (Cartersport)

Brian Morrison is presented with the County Motors Trophy by Denis Parkinson in 1988 at the last ever Beveridge Park races. (Ronnie Weir)

FRIDAY, 26th SEPTEMBER

350 c.c. Scratch Race.   **Event 1.**   **12.00 noon**

HEAT FINAL 1.

No.	Name	Machine	Placings	Time
1	D. Parkinson	Norton		
3	W. Doran	Norton		
4	W. S. Humphry	Norton		
5	W. McVeigh	Norton		
7	S. T. Barnett	Norton		
9	W. J. Mundy	Norton		
11	F. P. Heath	Norton		
14	S. M. Miller	Norton		
16	H. W. Billington	Norton		
18	L. A. Dear	Velocette		
20	F. Fairbairn	Norton		
21	A. E. Moule	Norton		
23	R. W. Thompson	Norton		
26	R. Pennycook	Norton		
29	R. R. Jeffery	Norton		
31	L. B. Ranson	Norton		

AWARDS FOR EVENT 1.

THE WHITAKER TROPHY (to be held from Meeting to Meeting or maximum of one year) kindly presented by H. A. Whitaker, Esq. of Scarborough, and

1. EIGHT POUNDS.
2. FIVE POUNDS.
3. FOUR POUNDS.
4. THREE POUNDS.

Denis Parkinson heads the entry list at Scarborough in 1947. (Cartersport)

CHAPTER SIXTEEN

THE 1971 SCOTT TRIAL

MALCOLM'S FIRST

Imagine a soccer match where you are tasked with marking Lionel Messi, play a three-ball round of golf with Rory McIlroy or face England's greatest fast bowler Jimmy Anderson steaming in with a new ball from the Kirkstall Lane End.

There are very few events left in the world where the average man (and increasingly woman) in the street can compete against the world's best, on equal terms, yet for over a hundred years, every autumn, a combination of 200 aspiring young rookies, experienced clubmen and the odd journeyman can assemble in the Richmondshire countryside to do battle with the sport's elite including the occasional World Champion thrown in.

The Scott Trial is one such place where all you need to take on twelve-times World Champion Dougie Lampkin is a decent trials machine, some protective gear, an ACU licence and pay the nominal entry fee. Plus, an ability to ride effortlessly through rocky streams, up almost vertical cliff faces and through man-devouring bogs over 80 miles without putting your foot down – it takes a special person, believe me.

The event began in 1914 when Alfred Scott, inventor and founder of the Scott Motorcycle Company, challenged the workers at his factory to ride from the factory in Shipley through the Yorkshire Dales to Burnsall near Grassington. Of the fourteen starters only nine finished. The event was reintroduced after the First World War in 1919 and although Alfred Scott died in 1923, the event continued to be run by the Scott workers until 1926.

Bradford and DMC took over and held 'The Scott' around Blubberhouses until 1938 when the permission to use the land was withdrawn meaning that a new home at Swainby was found for the immediate years after the Second World War. A reorganisation of boundaries by the ACU in 1950 saw a switch to Swaledale under the auspices of Darlington and DMC until 1990 when current custodians Richmond and DMC took over and continue to put on a wonderful event which has raised hundreds of thousands of pounds for local charities.

One of the most significant events was in 1971 when Yorkshireman Malcolm Rathmell got his hands on the Alfred Scott Memorial Trophy for the first time. Belfast legend Sammy Miller had taken victory on the moors around Swaledale and Arkengarthdale for the previous four years on his Spanish Bultaco, which had ended the British machine domination, but he was an absentee in 1971.

Malcolm Rathmell cleans Roan Splash on his way to victory at the 1971 Scott Trial. (Mortons Archive)

Rathmell, from Otley, had switched from motocross the year previously and had been drafted into the works Bultaco squad to continue the development of their revolutionary new bikes. Starting at number 185 out of the 186 entrants, which later became recognised as the most favourable due to later numbers giving competitors the best chance to set 'Standard Time' and also (allegedly) having an easier route through the sections due to earlier riders clearing a path, 'Rastus' as he was known, overcame a flat rear tyre for the final 6 miles, a broken back brake lever and a flooded engine to secure his first win ahead of fellow Yorkshireman Bill Wilkinson (the winner in 1964).

Back in those days, The Scott comprised a round of the British Trials Championship meaning points were up for grabs but despite Rathmell's victory, he would finish second in the title race behind Gordon Farley, who finished third on the day on his 250 cc Montesa.

Rathmell's winning tally of eighty-four marks lost (eighty-three on observation, one on time) compares to a total of twenty-six (twenty-one/five) incurred by 2022 Scott winner, Jack Price, on what is a similar course which starts near Feldom masts and goes round in a huge circle via Marske, Marrick, Reeth, Healaugh, Whaw, Langthwaite, Booze, Fremington and Helwith totalling around eighty sections.

Back in 1971, the course didn't include the dreaded Grouse Moor so was a little shorter meaning Alan R. C. (Sid) Lampkin's Standard Time of four hours, forty-one minutes and thirty-five seconds was slightly quicker compared to Jonathan Richardson's in 2022 of five hours and eighteen seconds, but the course nowadays is longer.

After 1971, Miller never added to his seven victories and for the next decade, apart from on two occasions when Pateley Bridge rider Rob Shepherd won in 1972 and Thornaby's Rob Edwards in 1974, the victories were shared between Rathmell and his nemesis, Martin Lampkin (Dougie's dad). Rathmell took his sixth and final victory in 1980 with Martin Lampkin's fourth and last win coming in 1982.

But the rider with the most wins is Graham Jarvis, who at one point was Malcolm's son-in-law, who took an unprecedented nine victories between 1996 and 2009. Dougie Lampkin needs another three to equal Jarvis' record but nowadays he's semi-retired and is helping the next generation as his sons Alfie and Fraiser are starting to make an impression on the sport these days.

The spirit of the event means it's still possible to park next to and rub shoulders with some of the sport's greatest on a windswept field in Swaledale. There are not many other places in the world you can do that.

Martin Lampkin exits the picturesque Orgate Falls section during the 1971 Scott Trial. (Nick Nicholls at Mortons Archive)

Dave Thorpe (Ossa) is followed by Bob Hutsby (Bultaco) at the popular Washfold Splash section in Hurst. (Nick Nicholls at Mortons Archive)

No.	Name	Machine	c.c.	Town
94.	C. Hedley	Bultaco	250	Westerhope
95.	M. Noyce	Triumph	500	Romsey
96.	B. L. Jennings	Cotton Cavalier	175	Mixenden
97.	Allan Whitby	Bultaco	250	Gilling West
98.	Norman Tiffen	Bultaco	250	Cockermouth
99.	D. C. Butcher	Bultaco	250	Shipley
100.	Colin Skinner	Montesa	250	Harrogate
101.	Philip Clarkson	Montesa	250	Leyland
102.	John Garside	Savage	125	West Melton
103.	D. C. Chick	Saracen	125	Taunton
104.	Robert Tyas	Bultaco Villiers	246	Barnsley
105.	Robert Smith	Montesa	247	Trawden
106.	Robert Knight	Bultaco	250	Kettering
107.	Mike Wilkinson	Greeves	175	Kettlewell
108.	Geoff Chandler	Bultaco	250	Nomansland
109.	Frank Lee	Bultaco	250	Bishop Auckland
110.	D. A. Onion	Cotton	170	Sherwood
111.	Roger Cain	Bultaco	250	Rainham
112.	Michael Collinson	Sprite	125	Doncaster
113.	Hugh S. Chew	Alta Suzuki	128	Skipton
114.	N. T. Hanks	B.S.A.	175	Streetley
115.	Peter Wetherill	Greeves	170	Thirsk
116.	John Pattinson	Greeves	170	Marske-by-the-Sea
117.	Jeff V. Smith	B.S.A.	250	Streetley
118.	E. Morris	Bultaco	250	South Shields
119.	D. V. Thornton	Bultaco	250	Haworth
120.	Stewart Wainwright	Montesa	247	Harrogate
121.	Richard T. Bainbridge	Montesa	247	Richmond
122.	K. G. Franklin	Bultaco	250	Ormskirk
123.	Robert M. Shepherd	Montesa	250	Pateley Bridge
124.	Arthur Redman	Greeves	252	Barnoldswick
125.	Malcolm Dennis	Montesa	250	Bedale
126.	Stewart Oughton	Montesa	247	Barkisland
127.	K. H. Coltman	Ossa	250	Thirsk
128.	Chris J. Catherall	Sprite	125	Liversedge
129.	Ian Haydon	Montesa	247	Exeter
130.	William Pye	Triumph	200	Ingleby Greenhow
131.	D. W. Hayes	Bultaco	250	North Gosforth
132.	Neil Cartwright			Bradford
133.	G. Monk	Heanes Bultaco	244	Farnham
134.	Jeff Ward	Montesa	247	Great Broughton
135.	Alan R. C. Lampkin	Bultaco	250	Silsden
136.	W. E. Breffit	Ossa	250	Nottingham
137.	John Bowlt	Bultaco	244	Stokesley
138.	R. Havelock	Bultaco	250	Eaglescliffe
139.	Arthur Lampkin	Bultaco	250	Silsden
140.	D. Ramplee	Bultaco	250	Southampton
141.	C. Kimber	Bultaco	244	Rochester
142.	Andrew P. Cooper	Bultaco	250	Sheffield
143.	Paul Jackson	Jackson Triumph	210	Huddersfield
144.	Michael Fawcett	Montesa	247	Br'pton-on-Swale
145.	Ken Saddington	KS	244	Great Broughton
146.	Rob Edwards	Montesa	250	Thornaby
147.	G. W. Simpson	Cotton	170	Wensley
148.	Dennis Hunter	Bultaco	244	Willington
149.	Bill Wilkinson	Ossa	250	Kettlewell
150.	Michael B. Stone	Montesa	247	Ryton-on-Tyne
151.	John Hemingway	Montesa	250	Leeds
152.	Thomas W. Alderson	Suzuki	125	Askrigg
153.	J. Ray Sayer	Triumph	500	Leyburn
154.	Paul Lowther	Dalesman Puch	125	Consett
155.	John Robert	Bultaco	247	Tilehurst
156.	Michael Bridger	Triumph	200	Crowborough
157.	Robert W. Griffiths	Bultaco	250	Dinas Powis
158.	Jim A. Sandiford	JAS Bultaco	244	Bury
159.	Richard J. Sunter	Montesa	247	Healaugh
160.	G. A. Greenland	Triumph	500	Liverstock
161.	G. R. Sharp	Bultaco	250	York
162.	Gordon Butterfield	Montesa	250	Consett
163.	D. J. Adsett	Greeves	175	Aldershot
164.	Graham Sanderson	Bultaco	250	Billy Row
165.	C. D. Singleton	Montesa	247	Kettering
166.	H. Martin Lampkin	Bultaco	250	Silsden
167.	C. A. Morewood	Bultaco	250	Sheffield
168.	A. C. Smith	Cotton	170	Nuneaton
169.	John Beecroft	Bultaco	250	Harrogate
170.	D. Spreight			Bradford
171.	Colin Smith	Bultaco	250	Coventry
172.	Norman W. Willis	Bultaco	250	Gilling West
173.	Mervyn Lavercombe	Saracen	125	Exeter
174.	Dave Smith	Bultaco	250	Birmingham
175.	Thomas Bingley	Bultaco	250	Milnthorpe
176.	Dennis Pitts	Ossa	250	Pudsey
177.	Frank McMullen	JAS Bultaco	244	Middleton (Lan.)
178.	Brian Johnson	Bultaco	244	Stokesley
179.	B. A. Williams	B.S.A.	250	Landford
180.	Thomas Robinson	Bultaco	244	Billy Row
181.	Dave Whinfield	Bultaco	250	South Shields
182.	Colin Hutchinson	Greeves	170	Huddersfield
183.	John Horsfall	Bultaco	244	Barrowford
184.	Andrew Gill	Bultaco	244	Worthington
185.	Malcolm Rathmell	Bultaco	250	Otley
186.	R. G. Bramham	Bultaco	250	Bramley

Some famous names on the 1971 entry list. (Cartersport)

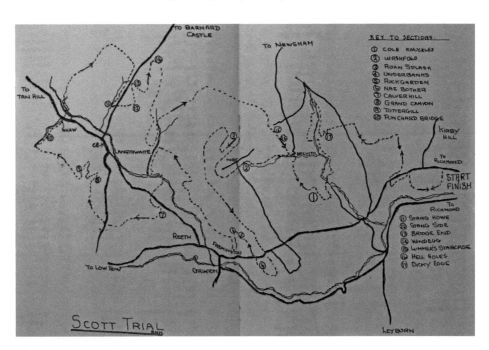

The route featured many of the sections still used today, some of which have been renamed. (Cartersport)

CHAPTER SEVENTEEN

YORKSHIRE RALLY LEGENDS

FOREST ADVENTURERS

When this book was being proposed, it went without saying that rallying would feature on a number of the pages. And so it has proved, with chapters pertaining to the sport, especially with the region being one of the most fertile grounds of the sport with some of the best stages in the world in the North Yorkshire Moors forests.

Of course, having such great venues on their doorstep, it was only natural that the local population would be involved and so a chapter was planned to feature some of the greatest competitors to come out of the white rose county.

It was to be entitled 'Yorkshire Rally Mafia' but during production, it emerged that another fellow Yorkshire motorsport enthusiast, Jonathan Pulleyn, had had a similar idea and had recently produced a wonderful hardbacked book entitled exactly that. In it he features twenty of Yorkshire's finest competitors and having read it, and spoken to 'JP', it's a fantastic read and if you enjoy this sort of thing, then I can thoroughly recommend it.

In truth, there are many more that could fill the pages of any motorsport book and whilst paying homage to the wonderful insight 'JP' gives, we'll do our best to pay tribute to some of the characters who have graced the stages over the years ourselves.

Number one has to be the erstwhile Steve Bannister, who, now in his seventies, epitomises the spirit of Yorkshire rallying. Born in Bridlington and since living all his life on the same farm near Malton, where for decades he has run a successful potato business, 'Banner' seems to be ageless.

His intimate knowledge of just about every corner, straight, jump and bump in the large swathe of tracks around Dalby, Cropton, Gale Rigg, Langdale and Staindale, and before them Wykeham, Harwood Dale, Broxa and Bickley, is almost encyclopaedic, and his results too numerous to list. Bannister also has a unique driving style, which sees him sitting so far forward, it's as if his nose is just about glued to the windscreen!

Although Steve has driven a few different makes over the years, the one car he's been synonymous with is the Ford Escort, particularly the Mk2 version, whereby each incarnation is usually dubbed 'Ethel' and the predominantly white colour scheme has been – and still is – interspersed with a distinct red stripe from bonnet to boot, in deference to his lifelong support for Manchester United.

Then there's octogenarian Robert Bean Esq. from Cleckheaton. 'Yumping Bob' to many, he has been competing since the 1950s and can still be found charging around the stages these days at a time of life when he really should be taking it a lot easier. Rumour has it that one time, he received his winter fuel allowance which he thanked the government for, saying it would buy him a set of rally tyres!

York's Peter 'Yuk' Hodgson – now there's a character. Anyone who has read his self-penned 'Fast Book' (along with some help from the aforementioned JP) can't help but be regaled by his antics and those of his service crew over the years. The 'craik' appeared to be most important with the actual competition secondary, but out on the stages, Yuk could certainly pedal his various charges, which, as well as Ford Escorts, included a Mini, Opel Manta, BMW, and a Triumph TR7.

Tony Fall from Bradford was one Yorkshireman who ended up becoming a professional rally driver and had much success in the 1970s. Born in March 1940, his competition career soon led to a drive in the BMC works team alongside Paddy Hopkirk, Timo Mäkinen and 'The Rally Professor', Rauno Aaltonen.

Fall also drove for British Leyland Cars in an Austin 1800 in the 1968 London to Sydney Rally, which was followed two years later by him competing in the 1970 London to Mexico World Cup Rally where his co-driver was England footballer Jimmy Greaves. The pair finished sixth.

Other famous Yorkshiremen include road rallying legend Ron Beecroft from Harrogate and Tony Drummond from York, who followed a hugely successful motorcycle grass track career with both stage rallying and rallycross.

Top co-drivers too came from the region in the shape of John Millington, originally from Pudsey but latterly living near York, and Ilkley's Phil Short, whose list of British and World Championship successes are as long as they are impressive, prior to a spell in team management. Short's various steeds over a long and successful career read like a 'who's who' of rallying including Bjorn Waldegård, Hannu Mikkola, Walter Röhrl, Pentti Airikkala and David Llewellyn, which led to a total of seventeen international victories.

York's David 'Piggy' Thompson was a top competitor whose son James was twice British Touring Car champion and also had a stint at rallying and likewise renowned Bradford car dealer Jack Tordoff, whose grandson Sam found success in the world of circuit racing. Peter Smith from Hull is another pathfinding rally driver whose son Guy combines a successful rally career with that of being a Le Mans 24 Hours winner too.

The list is endless with names such as John Heppenstall from Elland, Mike Jackson from Driffield and more latterly, the likes of Warren Philliskirk, Pete Slights and Andy Elliott from York, along with Castleton's Ryan Champion all making some sort of impression on the sport. Indeed, Mike Taylor Developments in Northallerton even ran Ford's World Championship team in the 1990s with the likes of Carlos Sainz, Stig Andervang, and Krzysztof Hołowczyc being regulars in the odd restaurant in the market town when visiting on business.

Tony Fall was one of the most successful drivers, seen here on the 1971 Welsh Rally in his Datsun 240Z. (Rally Retro)

Bob Bean has been competing since the 1950s and can still be found on the stages today well into his eighties. (Rally Retro)

Yuk Hodgson has driven a wide variety of cars over the years, including a Mini on the snowy 1979 Mintex Rally. (Rally Retro)

David 'Piggy' Thompson makes a splash on the 1977 Mintex Rally. (Rally Retro)

Steve Bannister charges past the masses of spectators on the 1980 Mintex Rally. (Rally Retro)

CHAPTER EIGHTEEN

THE WAINMAN STOCK CAR DYNASTY

KEEPING IT IN THE FAMILY

Fifty years and three generations, that is how embedded in stock car racing Silsden's Wainman family is.

The legacy began in the 1960s when Frankie Wainman Senior visited the Nelson Stadium to watch the BriSCA Stock Car Racing and made the decision he wanted to be part of it. Frankie spent three weeks constructing his own car to compete in before making his debut at Rochdale Stadium in 1970 emblazoned with the number 212.

He had made the top grade (at the time) of Star by 1972 after grabbing his first heat win and climbing the handicap system. His first final win followed in 1973 at Nelson Stadium, the place that inspired him, and he was soon catching the attention of spectators and becoming a fans' favourite.

In 1976 he was included in the sport's inaugural Superstars grade, a position he held for a record-breaking ten consecutive years. As the decade changed Frankie, nicknamed 'Smiler' due to his infectious smile, found himself developing a friendly rivalry with Stuart 'The Maestro' Smith on track, with fans supporting either one or the other but never both drivers.

He continued to entertain crowds up until 2007 and collected nearly every accolade in the sport at both world and national levels. He still supports his family and Wainman Racing today. Frankie's eldest son Frankie Junior then decided to follow in his father's footsteps and take up the sport in 1987 at just sixteen years old. He still races as Frankie Wainman Junior (and is often referred to in commentary as Junior Wainman) and took the number 515.

Frankie Junior also built his own car to get into the sport and soon became a top name in his own right as he was winning heats and finals within weeks of starting. There is nothing that Wainman Junior has not won in BriSCA Formula One and he was crowned World Champion in 1998, 2005 and 2016 and is a nine-time British Champion. He has also taken the Silver Roof fourteen times and has also developed the FWJ Racing workshop, a car-building business, further cementing the family's name in the sport by building cars for many of the other competitors.

When Frankie Wainman Senior decided to call it a day in 2007 after thirty-eight years in stock car racing, he handed his 212 number down to his sixteen-year-old son Daniel, who made his BriSCA Formula One debut later that year at his father's testimonial meeting. Success began to come for him in 2008 as he rose up the ranks to Star grade and finished that year with the World of Shale title.

Around this time the two Wainman sons, Daniel and Frankie Junior, found history repeating itself as they were racing closely against Andy and Stuart Smith Junior, the sons of Stuart Smith, who had been their father's arch-rival. This attracted the attention of the national media and found itself being the subject of a BBC TV series as the Wainman family were followed by a filming crew for a whole year in 2009 for a documentary about the famous Smith versus Wainman rivalry.

Gears and Tears was aired in 2010 on BBC One with millions of viewers tuning in and in-turn promoting the sport and drawing in new fans. As a result, the 2010 BriSCA Formula One World Championship event in Coventry saw the largest crowd stock car racing had seen for a decade.

Frankie Junior continues to race today and in 2022 was crowned European Champion for the fourth time at Odsal Stadium in Bradford. He just missed out on a further world title when in the deciding round he slid out after being caught by some oil from another car, but he recovered to take fourth place.

Frankie Wainman Senior's grandchildren, thus Frankie Junior's children, are now taking over the family 'business' with Phoebe and Frankie Junior Junior (JJ) starting their careers in the sport in 2011 and they continue to compete today alongside and against their dad.

Phoebe is the only female driver to get into the national shoot-out for the Silver Roof accolade, but after qualifying, she did not quite manage to claim it over the ten decider

It all started with Frankie Wainman Senior, but it wasn't all glory in the early days! (Wainman Collection)

meetings. She finished second to her dad in the 2022 European Championship Final whilst Frankie JJ was third in an historic result.

Frankie JJ and Phoebe also headed to the 2022 World Cup in Venray along with Frankie Junior. Frankie Junior finished fifth with Phoebe two places behind in seventh. Frankie JJ has had his fair share of bad luck over the years. Both him and Phoebe were hoping to qualify for the 2022 World Final in Ipswich, but they failed to make it into the feature race.

What with the Lampkin's success on two wheels, there's something about successful motorsporting families coming from Silsden!

Frankie Wainman Junior in action at Northampton in 1990. (Wainman Collection)

Typical action from Frankie Junior in car 515. (Ian Bannister)

Frankie celebrates his world title win at Ipswich in 2022. (Ian Bannister)

The Muddy Wainmans! Frankie JJ, Phoebe and Frankie Junior after a particularly wet meeting on the shale. (Ian Bannister)

CHAPTER NINETEEN

RUFFORTH AND ELVINGTON

THE YORK CONTINGENT

The cathedral city of York is the historic county town of Yorkshire with its origins going back to Roman times, founded as Eboracum in AD 71. The city was built at the confluence of the rivers Ouse and Foss and has long-standing buildings and other structures, including a minster, a castle, and city walls. Famed for being the home of Rowntree and Terry's confectionary, it also used to have two motor racing tracks.

In fact, the origins of motorsport in York can be traced back to Speedway in the 1930s. The track in the Burnholme Estate was completed in 1930 and a demonstration event staged. In 1931 the track staged team and open events and the York team took part in the National Trophy. The Knavesmire, famous as the home of York racecourse nowadays, also hosted Speed Trials from 1923 to 1927. Loaned to the ACU Yorkshire Centre by the Corporation of the City of York, the annual events were run in aid of raising funds for local hospitals.

Rufforth lies about 4 miles west of York and is mentioned in the Domesday Book. On the close outskirts stood RAF Rufforth, which was a purpose-built bomber airfield constructed during 1941 and which opened in June 1942 for use by Operational Training Units and later a Heavy Conversion Unit flying Halifax bombers.

It eventually closed in 1959 but was retained as an emergency landing ground but like many dormant airfield sites, Rufforth lent itself to the burgeoning motorsport scene so in March that year, the British Racing and Sports Car Club held the very first race meeting there.

Under the approval of the Station Commander, another one soon followed in May 1959, which featured Jim Clark, who won the sports car race in a Lister Jaguar. Racing continued into the 1960s with drivers visiting from all over the country but one of the problems was the main straight was deemed too long. Many of the clubmen's engines wouldn't survive the entirety so the straight was shortened and the track length reduced from 2.1 miles to a more manageable 1.7 miles.

The site remained in RAF hands until they finally departed in 1974 but its purpose as a racetrack could only be served after considerable efforts of a working party of organisers who, for every meeting, had to build the circuit using removable ARMCO barriers, as well as miles of chestnut fencing to contain the hordes of spectators, and then take it all down afterwards. This continued throughout the decade and into the 1970s where one of the feature meetings was the 'Battle of Britain', which Rufforth shared with nearby Croft.

By 1973, the early origins of health and safety protocols were starting to be implemented and such regulations had an impact on the finances of the clubs that run events. But with limited resources and dwindling interest, by 1977 the end was in sight and Rufforth hosted its final race meeting in September of that year. In July 1981, the site was sold and is now the home of the York Gliding Centre and a microlight flying club.

On the other side of the city was another unique venue which was unlike most other race circuits, apart from sharing the same logistics as Rufforth in as much as the track had to be built and then dismantled after every race meeting.

The village of Elvington is around 7 miles to the south-east of York and has a proud history of motorsport. Originating as a grass airfield, in the early 1940s it was entirely reconstructed with three hardened runways replacing the grass. It reopened in October 1942 as a station for 77 Squadron RAF and saw a squadron of Handley Page Halifax four-engined heavy bombers stationed there. Despite considerable losses, it played a major part in the Battle of the Ruhr and the bombing of Berlin.

Latterly, Elvington was the only airfield in the United Kingdom used by the remainder of the Free French Forces, who also flew Halifax bombers until they moved to Bordeaux in October 1945 where they became the basis for the new Air Force of liberated France. In September 1957, a memorial was unveiled in Elvington village dedicated to the two French squadrons.

After the war, control of the 400-acre airfield was transferred to RAF Maintenance Command until 1952 when it was greatly enlarged and extended for use by the United States Air Force and boasted two of the longest runways in the country.

The first race circuit at Elvington was established in July 1962 where the British Racing and Sports Car Club (BRSCC) ran a meeting on a 1.7-mile course, all contained within the massive dispersal square. Tony Lanfranchi set a number of lap records that day before another car meeting took place on 8 July 1962 and was reported by *Autosport*, which said that the BRSCC hoped to run a further meeting a year later.

In June 1964, the first of what would become an established activity at Elvington took place with a weekend dedicated to setting speed records. Such was the length and width of the runways, they lent themselves favourably to high-speed runs and these continued for many years.

Motorcycle racing can be traced back to August 1969 where over 7,000 spectators witnessed Yorkshireman Tony Jefferies take victory in the main race over the 1.9-mile track with various local clubs, including the Auto 66 Club, hosting additional events. By 1971, national races were being organised, which attracted over 400 riders, including stars of the future such as Mick Grant and Barry Sheene.

Bike racing, and other occasional motorsporting activities, continued right the way through to the 2000s but nowadays activities are restricted to the occasional speed record meeting and a driving experience centre, as well as the venue hosting the Yorkshire Air Museum.

Straw bales mark out the track as the Formula Ford action takes place at Rufforth. (Tony Todd)

Elvington is synonymous with world record attempts. Chris Bartram launches his 750 cc Norton down the strip in October 1970. (Nick Nicholls at Mortons Archive)

Elvington, July 1962, saw J. H. Haynes win the first race of the day in his Lotus 7. (Cartersport)

A rare aerial shot of the wide-open expanse of Elvington with the racetrack permutations visible. (Neil Whitley)

CHAPTER TWENTY

THE GINETTA STORY

YORKSHIRE'S SPORTS CAR

Ginetta began its story back in 1958 when it was founded by brothers Bob, Ivor, Trevers and Douglas Walklett with a vision of 'a race car for the road' and was originally based in Suffolk, which of course is a bit of a distance from Yorkshire.

The first product was a glass fibre body shell that was designed to be fitted to a Ford 6.0 or 7.5-kw chassis. From there the Ginetta G1 was developed based on a pre-war Wolseley Hornet six and was not destined for production.

The first car, the G2, was built as a kit car for enthusiasts. The tubular frame chassis was designed to take Ford components and an aluminium body with around a hundred being produced. In 1959 the G3 was manufactured followed by the G4, which was designed to be used as an everyday car but was still utilised in motorsport. It had a new Ford 105E engine and a glass fibre GT-style body along with updated coil springing suspension at the front with a Ford live axle at the rear.

In 1962 the firm moved to Witham, Essex, again a considerable distance from Yorkshire, where it remained until 1988, although it had temporarily moved to larger premises in Sudbury in Suffolk between 1972 and 1974.

A coupe variant of the G4 followed in 1961, which got up to 120 mph in road tests, but production halted in 1968 after around 500 units had been made with a range of Ford engines. It was revived in 1981 with the Series IV that was slightly larger and with a new chassis.

In 1965 the Ginetta G10 was launched at the Racing Car Show, intending to be more powerful than its predecessors. A prototype of the car, fitted with a 4.7-litre V8 Ford Mustang engine, won its debut race at Brands Hatch with works driver Chris Meek behind the wheel. But the firm had failed to make a homologated version of the car to keep it in competition so after production of just three cars it was forced into retirement. Ginetta then produced a road version of the G10, the G11, which had an MGB 1800 cc engine instead of the Ford V8.

The first complete Ginetta car was sold between 1967 and 1974 after the G15 was fully type approved. Eight hundred were made over the seven years with eight being labelled Super S as they were produced with Volkswagen engines.

The firm's move to Scunthorpe (a little nearer) in the late 1980s allowed Ginetta to expand following reorganisation and they also began making cars in kit form again starting with the G27. The Walkletts then sold the business in November 1989 to a group of enthusiasts based in Sheffield, seeing Ginetta, alas, taking its first step into Yorkshire and leading to the four founding brothers retiring.

Managing Director Martin Phaff went on to run Ginetta as they produced the Ginetta G20 and Ginetta G33. It was during this period that the brand moved towards being viewed as a racing car company as opposed to a kit car manufacturer as the improved G27 saw them venture into the one-make racing series as the Ginetta Championship began supporting the National GT Championship.

As financial difficulties later fell upon Phaff and the company, racing car driver, engineer, and businessman Lawrence Tomlinson and his LNT Automotive company acquired the business in 2005. He shared the aims of the founders: to produce innovative, capable, and great value sports cars.

Tomlinson moved the business in mid-2007 to a factory at Garforth near Leeds, aiming to sell 200 cars per year. He designed the base specification for the successful Ginetta G50, marking the fiftieth anniversary of the company. Using a 3.5-litre V6 engine, in 2007 the car completed its first race in the European GT4 Cup in Nogaro, France, where it finished second. It was then officially launched at Autosport International in 2008 alongside the Ginetta G50 GT4. Together the cars have become Ginetta's best sellers with race wins including the Dubai 24 Hour Endurance Race in 2012 with Optimum Motorsport.

In 2008 the Ginetta G50 Cup was born, supporting the British Formula Three Championship and British GT Championship before it made the switch in 2009 to support the British Touring Car Championship (BTCC).

In March 2010 Ginetta, under Tomlinson, expanded further, as it took over Somerset-based sports car manufacturer Farbio and inherited their F400. A year later the G55 was launched and with its introduction the Ginetta G50 Cup was reborn as the Michelin Ginetta GT4 Supercup before the G60 came along powered by a Ford-sourced 3.7-litre V6 engine.

Ginetta has run various racing series in recent years as it has grown its motorsport presence. The Ginetta GT5 Challenge supported the British GT Championship since its inception in 2011 whilst the Ginetta Junior Championship, the UK's longest-running junior series, has become synonymous with grassroots motorsport, supporting the BTCC since 2008. It sees drivers aged between fourteen and seventeen years old compete, initially using the Ginetta G20 but in 2010 Tomlinson brought in the newer, safer G40J car to the series.

Following its success, the popular Ginetta G40 Challenge car was introduced for adults to use in the Challenge series, and it led to the unveiling of Ginetta's second road car, the Ginetta G40R in 2011.

Ginetta has now cut its ties supporting the BTCC and as of 2023 the Ginetta Junior series will support the British GT package whilst the GT4 Supercup has been scrapped. Two further categories will run alongside the British GT; the entry level Ginetta GT Academy, launched in 2021, and the all-new Ginetta GT championship featuring two main classes, the GT Pro and GT5.

It has also developed the LMP3 prototype endurance car that is used for the European Le Mans Series, Asian Le Mans Series and the IMSA Prototype Challenge. It launched the

LMP1 in 2014 as the model dominated European competition in 2015 as three different Ginettas won all five races in the European Le Mans Series.

Ginetta has continued to evolve its offering over recent times. It invested further in its future commitment to motorsport by buying Blyton Park test circuit near Gainsborough in 2017 where it develops road and racing cars. They also run the Ginetta track days and experiences from the Lincolnshire venue, whilst in 2019 flagship supercar the Akula was also launched at the Geneva Motor Show.

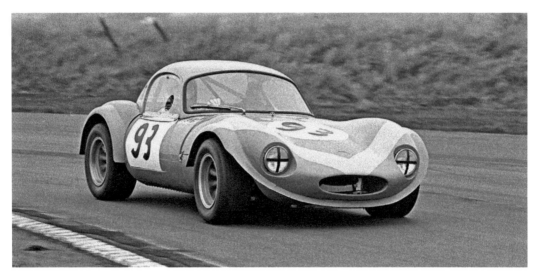

John Absalom had lots of success in the 1960s and 1970s in a Ginetta G4 at Croft. (Tony Todd)

John Absalom in action again at Croft in the Ginetta G4. (Tony Todd)

Triple W Series champion Jamie Chadwick started her career in Ginetta Juniors in 2014. (Jakob Ebrey)

So too did current Formula One star Lando Norris, seen here leading the field in 2014. (Jakob Ebrey)

Yorkshireman Max Coates has also dabbled with Ginettas during his promising career, here driving in the Protyre GT5 series. (Jakob Ebrey)

ACKNOWLEDGEMENTS

The author and publisher would like to thank the following people/organisations for permission to use copyright material in this book:

Tony Todd
Nick Nicholls at Mortons Archive
Jane Skayman & Jonathan Schofield (Mortons Archive)
Terry and Yvonne Wright
Ian Bannister
David Bell
Chris Binns
Alan Carter
Double Red Photographic
Michael Dowkes
Jakob Ebrey
Andy Ellis
Alan Horner
Sarah Hall
Charlotte Jobling
Fergus McAnallan – Rally Retro
Jonathan Pulleyn – Yorkshire Rally Mafia
Jonathan Smith – Environmental Photography
Neil Sturgeon
David Tearle
Tracy Thompson
Miss Jean Wade (1931–2023)
Phil Wain
Ronnie Weir
The staff at Amberley Publishing
Various other publishers and contributors no matter how small

As with the first book we produced, *North Eastern Motorsport: A Century of Memories*, every attempt has been made to seek permission for copyright material used in this book. However, if we have inadvertently used copyright material without permission/acknowledgement we apologise and we will make the necessary correction at the first opportunity.

This book would not have been possible without the help from many kind and knowledgeable people who have gladly volunteered assistance when called upon.

Firstly, the main photographic source being my good friend Tony Todd whose wonderful archive has been a massive part of this project and I'm grateful for his unstinting help and support yet again. Every time I've tasked him with a list of requirements, he has responded immediately and once again, this book wouldn't have been possible without his contributions.

Fellow lifelong motorsport enthusiasts Terry Wright and his wife Yvonne have again been a wonderful mine of information and supplied many pictures also. They too have gone above and beyond the call of duty to oblige with my seemingly endless requests.

The fantastic Mortons Archive, and in particular Jane Skayman and Jonathan Schofield, who have happily supplied a number of rare images for inclusion within these pages, many of which have never been published before. I can always rely on them to furnish my obscure requirements and we have a wonderful working relationship going back many years.

In particular, I am grateful too for the help of Amanda Cornforth-Smith who helped me get the book over the line in the time we had available. ACS and I go back a long way and as well as our journalistic associations, she has even agreed to co-drive for me on many rallies. She is a fierce and talented rally driver in her own right and she and her family are staunch motorsport supporters.

There are numerous photographers and suppliers of information listed earlier and I thank each and every one of them. All have responded favourably with requests and hopefully this book showcases their talents and enthusiasm. A big thank you to Ashleigh Morris too who has assisted with proofreading this project once again, as well as a number of other jobs I've tasked her with during recent times. She has worked late into the night many times to ensure the copy is readable.

Once again, a special acknowledgement goes to Hannah Chapman of the *Darlington and Stockton Times*, whose encouragement for me to contribute a few trips down the motorsporting memory lane during the difficult period of 'lockdowns', which she kindly published, led to this idea to do something more substantial, and included within these pages are a reflection of some of those events.

Auntie Jean's programmes have once again been consulted along with her newspaper and magazine cuttings, which have been instrumental in ensuring we get the facts right. In particular, the ultra-rare programmes from the 1938 Scott Trial and 1946 Oliver's Mount meetings are worth their weight in gold – to me at least. Sadly, she passed away just before this book was published but I'll cherish our reminiscing about the 'good old days' and I am deeply grateful to her (and Uncle Les) for encouraging my interest in all things motorsport, which has become a lifelong passion.

Also, there have been so many people who I have run ideas past and asked for help; invariably I'll forget someone so if that person is you, I sincerely apologise.

Like the previous one, this book is also dedicated to my wife Sue, who for nearly forty years has unstintingly supported the various sporting and business challenges I have undertaken, and without whose help the many things in life I have achieved would simply not have been possible.

Finally, a special thanks to Steve Webster MBE for agreeing to write the foreword. He and I are of a similar age and raced at a similar time, on similar circuits and lived only a few miles apart. And whereas I can boast a handful of club championships, he went on to be, in my opinion, the greatest sidecar racer of all time, winning no fewer than ten World Championships.

Thanks for buying a copy of this book. I hope you enjoy it as much as I enjoyed writing it, and here's to many more wonderful motorsporting memories in the future.

Larry Carter
Northallerton, North Yorkshire

The author interviewing World Superbike champion James Toseland. (Double Red)